CONTENTS

SCOPE AND SEQUENCE

Speaking of Values 2
Conversation and Listening

Robin Mills

PEARSON
Longman

Speaking of Values 2: Conversation and Listening

Pearson Education, 10 Bank Street, White Plains, NY 10606

Staff credits: The people who made up the *Speaking of Values 2* team,
representing editorial, production, design, and manufacturing, are: Christine Edmonds,
Diana George, Laura Le Dréan, Amy McCormick, Shana McGuire,
Martha McGaughey, Joan Poole, Edith Pullman, and Patricia Wosczyk.

Cover design: Patricia Woszyk
Cover illustration: Susan Detrich
Text design: Patricia Wosczyk
Text composition: Laserwords
Text font: Minion

Text credits: **p. 8,** Austin Cline, based on several articles from about.com:
"Someone Could Be Tracking Your Every Move!," "RFID Tags: Fearing the Future,"
"Tracking Everything, Everywhere, All The Time," "What are RFID Tags?" (no date);
p. 21, Jim Brancher, "Integrity Matters." Reprinted with permission of *The Salinas Californian*,
December 15, 2004; **p. 33,** "Buying More: Why Numerical Signs Make You Overspend at the
Grocery Store" reprinted with permission of Food and Brand Lab www.foodpsychology.com
Champaign, Illinois (no date); **p. 42,** Joyce Rothschild, "Whistle-Blowers' Concern About
Retaliation Justified," Virginia Tech Summer 2002; **p. 53,** Steve Brennan, "Reality TV: Viewers
worldwide are tuning in to Reality TV. Cable channel content varies from country to country."
Hollywood Reporter. Los Angeles, January 5, 2004. © Copyright. Reuters. All rights reserved.
Distributed by Valeo IP. **p. 63,** Ann Svensen "School Uniforms: Quick Fix or Bad Call?"
Permission granted by www.FamilyEducation.com © 2000–2004 Pearson Education, Inc.
All Rights Reserved. **p. 75,** Peter Josty, "Billionaires Are a Dime a Dozen," *Calgary Herald*,
July 6, 2001; **p. 86,** "Boomerang Kids Don't Have to Be a Financial Drain: Establishing
Ground Rules Makes all the Difference," Englewood, Colorado, August 19, 2003. © 2004,
National Endowment for Financial Education. Adapted with permission. All rights reserved;
p. 96, Nona Yates, "Their New Retirement Community: The Net; Retirees ease loneliness
with computers." *Los Angeles Times,* September 8, 1997; **pp. 107–108,** David Selley,
"IKEA in the News," Ethics Centre: Canadian Centre for Ethics and Corporate Policy.
Toronto, Ontario, Canada, February 2000. **pp. 119–121,** Laura Beil "Mind Makeovers:
Want to play chess better? Neurological upgrades could be around the corner,"
The Dallas Morning News, November 1, 2004. Reprinted with permission of the
Dallas Morning News. **p. 133,** Charles Hawley, "Rome Loses Some Traditional Flavor,"
Christian Science Monitor, Rome, August 11, 2004.

Illustrations: Dusan Petricic

Photo credits: **p. 3** (left) © Ress Meyer/Corbis, (right) © Lester Lefkowitz/Corbis;
p. 14 © Jim Cummins/Corbis; **p. 20** © Reuters/Corbis; **p. 48** (top) © Royalty-Free/Corbis,
(bottom left) Andrea Comas/Reuters/Corbis, (bottom right) © Yang Lei/Associated Press;
p. 58 (top) © Catherine Karnow/Corbis, (bottom) © Daniel Bosler/Getty Images;
p. 68 (left) © Ralf Schultheiss/Corbis, (right) © John Madere/Corbis; **p. 71** © Reuters/Corbis;
p. 126 © Dave G. Houser/Corbis; **p. 127** © Don Conrad/Corbis; **p. 132** © Michael S. Yamashita/Corbis.

Library of Congress Cataloging-in-Publication Data

Mills, Robin, 1962-
  Speaking of values 2 / Robin Mills.
     p. cm.
   ISBN 0-13-182547-X (student book : alk. paper) -- ISBN 0-13-141174-8 (audio CD)
   1. English language--Textbooks for foreign speakers.   2. English language--
Spoken English--Problems, exercises, etc.   3. Listening--Problems, exercises, etc.
I. Title.   II. Title: Speaking of values two.
PE1128.M5865 2005
428.2'4--dc22
                                                                    2005009333

Printed in the United States of America
  7 8 9 10 V001 13 12 11

Conversation Tip	Beyond the Classroom
Using enthusiasm to persuade/ Responding to someone else's idea	Write a short essay about your views on privacy and privacy protections.
Leading and taking part in discussions	Write an essay: Should sports figures be role models?
Saying "no" to a salesperson	Write a description of an ad. Analyze your views about advertising and consumer rights.
Confronting a difficult situation	Watch and respond to a movie about whistleblowers.
Expressing disapproval	Develop a reality TV show.
Speaking about disappointment	Research the history of tattoos and write a short essay about them.
Showing and responding to surprise or disbelief	1. Research a billionaire. 2. Imagine you have 10 minutes to talk to a billionaire: What would you ask?
Expressing determination	Write a personal essay: Who should take care of the elderly?
Giving your perspective	1. Write a diary entry. What would your life be like without high-tech communications? 2. Research the effects of spam.
Job interviews	1. Research companies that invest to improve the public good. 2. What benefits should a CEO offer to employees?
Talking to your doctor before surgery	Research a controversial medical procedure and write an essay describing its pros and cons.
Describing a process	1. Write an essay about artifact removal: What should be done? 2. Research a United Nations–designated World Heritage site. Give an oral report.

PREFACE

Speaking of Values 2 is aimed at encouraging high-intermediate students to address and discuss real-life problems. For example:

- *Your company throws away old computers. One of your colleagues has been taking those computers and selling them on eBay. Another colleague tells the president of the company about this, and the first one loses his job. How do you feel about the informer? Why?*

- *You are going to a formal affair but don't have enough money to buy an appropriate outfit. A friend suggests that you buy something suitable, wear it to the event, and return it to the store afterwards. What do you do?*

- *You take the train to and from work every day. You really enjoy this quiet time to read and relax. One day you are reading a very good book. The person behind you is having a loud conversation on her cell phone. She is talking to her friend about some very personal information that you do not want to hear. What do you do?*

Such issues encourage students to compare their ideas and values with those of classmates with other backgrounds, personalities, and cultures. Because there are no right or wrong answers to these questions, students lose their fear of being wrong, and concentrate on using English to discuss ideas and develop critical thinking skills.

In the past decade, new ideas have emerged about language teaching. While we still acknowledge the benefits of interactive activities based on motivating content, we also realize the value of systematic use of language-focused exercises in the classroom. The difference between weaker and stronger students, after the basic level, is often a difference of lexical ability. Stronger students appear more fluent because they have a greater variety of phrases at the tips of their tongues. The most efficient way to develop this fluency in the classroom is to select expressions and phrases in context and then focus on practicing them in meaningful and enjoyable ways.

In addition, there has been an increased emphasis on listening comprehension skill, not just as an aid to better speaking, but also as a way of understanding language that is more complex than the language a student can produce. For some people, understanding English is as challenging as speaking it.

Speaking of Values 2 incorporates these ideas by including a lexical segment and a complete listening component.

Each unit of *Speaking of Values 2* contains the following sections:

THINKING ABOUT THE TOPIC

Photos and illustrations are followed by questions to get students interested in a topic and activate their knowledge of it.

TALKING ABOUT YOUR EXPERIENCE

Students first answer a set of questions based on personal experience and then ask a classmate the same questions. The discussion questions that follow draw from and build on these questions, but are more open-ended.

LISTENING

Each listening task involves an issue that relates the unit subject. For example, the listening in Unit 4, Why Blow the Whistle? raises the question of what to do if you find out that the company you work for is illegally dumping toxic chemicals. In Unit 12, Cultural Heritage vs. Modernization, the listening deals with the problem of large corporations moving in near cultural monuments and displacing local merchants.

Warm-up questions prepare the students for what they will hear. Each listening is followed by comprehension questions and discussion questions.

WORDS AND PHRASES ABOUT THE TOPIC

Students learn words and phrases about the topic through fill-in-the-blank, matching, and multiple-choice exercises. Each section also includes an activity where students use the words in context.

PROBLEM SOLVING

As in *Speaking of Values 1,* Problem Solving remains at the heart of the text. Students consider problems that are difficult to answer because there are two or more sides to the question. They read or listen to the problem. They choose a solution and explain their reasons orally or in writing. Then, working in small groups, they come to an agreement on a solution.

In Speaking of Values 2, the problems are recorded, giving the teacher more options in using the material. Students can listen with their books closed, or they can listen, write the problem, and check what they've written by comparing their version to the one in the book. As another alternative, they can listen to the problem and try to come up with a possible solution before looking at the choices in the book.

FROM THE NEWS

Students read authentic news articles. Follow-up questions help them practice comprehension of main ideas, words, and phrases from context and inference. A final set of questions asks students to express their opinions.

WORDS AND PHRASES

Students learn words and phrases that are related to the topic, often items that have been taken directly from the Problem Solving or From the News sections. Short quizzes based on words and phrases from each unit are included in the *Teacher's Pack,* and can be photocopied for classroom use.

CONVERSATION TIP

Students learn high-frequency phrases and language functions that will be useful in the following Act It Out section.

ACT IT OUT

Students do a role play that relates to the Unit's theme, learning useful functions such as making suggestions, expressing likes and dislikes, giving advice, and explaining consequences. Unlike many of the other sections of the book, this one does not require students to express their opinions. Rather, they become actors who learn parts and improvise in any way they wish.

PROVERBS OR SAYINGS

Students read and discuss proverbs or sayings related to the theme of each Unit. They are encouraged to give examples that illustrate the meanings of the proverbs and to share similar sayings from their own cultures.

BEYOND THE CLASSROOM

A homework assignment asks students to bring to class information they've gathered from the Internet, the library, people outside the class, or other sources, and report to the class. Motivated students can produce amazing results and become an inspiration to others.

APPENDIX

The appendix contains an index of the vocabulary and language functions presented and practiced in the text.

AUDIO CDs

The Listening, Problem Solving and From the News sections have been recorded on CDs. The symbol ⌒ appears next to these activities. Audioscripts for recorded material that does not appear in the text can be found in the *Teacher's Pack*.

TEACHER'S PACK

A separate *Teacher's Pack* includes teaching suggestions for each section, quizzes for each Unit, the answer key for the quizzes, the Student Book answer key, and audioscripts for the Listening, Problem Solving, and From the News sections.

REVIEWERS FOR *SPEAKING OF VALUES 2*

Leslie Jo Adams, Santa Ana College, Santa Ana, CA; **Lauren Brombert,** DePaul University, Chicago, IL; **Christina Cavage,** Atlantic Cape Community College, Atlantic City, NJ; **Carol Deemer,** Elgin Community College, Elgin, IL; **Steve Gras,** Plattsburgh State University of New York, Plattsburgh, NY; **Julie Gunzelman Un,** Massasoit Community College, Brockton, MA; **Mary Hill,** North Shore Community College, Danvers, MA; **Diane Mahin,** University of Miami, Coral Gables, FL; **Catherine Nameth,** University of Massachusetts, Northampton, MA; **David Ross,** Houston Community College, Houston, TX; **Randy Schafer,** Tokyo, Japan; **Barbara Smith-Palinkas,** University of South Florida, Tampa, FL; **Carol Swett,** Benedictine University, Lisle, IL; **Paul Thomas,** DePaul University, Chicago, IL; **Marcos Valle,** Edmonds Community College, Lynnwood, WA; **Linda Wells,** University of Washington, Seattle, WA; **Cynthia Wiseman,** LaGuardia Community College, New York, NY.

ACKNOWLEDGMENTS

I would like to thank the many people at Pearson who were instrumental in developing, editing, and producing the material in *Speaking of Values 2:* Laura Le Dréan, Dena Daniels, Amy McCormick, Joan Poole, and Diana George. Thanks are also due to Irene Schoenberg for creating *Speaking of Values 1* and offering her ideas for *Speaking of Values 2*. In addition, I would like to thank my colleague and friend Shalle Leeming for her creative input.

ABOUT THE AUTHOR

Robin Mills is a California native and has lived in the San Francisco Bay Area since 1987. In 1993, she received a Master's in Teaching English as a Second Language from San Francisco State University. She has taught in a variety of settings, including University of San Francisco, City College of San Francisco, Mills College, and the American Language Institute in San Francisco, California. She most recently taught ESL to deaf students at City College of San Francisco. She is also an author of *Northstar: Listening/Speaking* Basic/Low Intermediate, *Northstar Reading and Writing Activity Book,* Basic/Low Intermediate and *Prime Time, Future Time* and *Real Time English* workbooks written by Michael Rost.

UNIT 1

Is Your Privacy Really Private?

THINKING ABOUT THE TOPIC

Talk in small groups or with the whole class.

1. What's happening in each picture? How are the people reacting? Are they angry or upset? Why do they feel this way?

2. Have you had any of these experiences? What happened? What did you do?

TALKING ABOUT YOUR EXPERIENCE

People have different views about privacy. What kinds of personal information are you willing to share with others? What kinds of personal information do you believe in keeping private?

Read the Personal Information column in the chart below. How do you feel about each item? Rate your feelings from 1 to 5, with 1 being "not very private" and 5 being "very private." Circle the number that best represents the degree of privacy you prefer. Be ready to discuss your reasoning.

Personal Information	Not Very Private ← → Very Private				
My phone number	1	2	3	4	5
My religion	1	2	3	4	5
My bank account number	1	2	3	4	5
My favorite color	1	2	3	4	5
My feelings	1	2	3	4	5
My marital status	1	2	3	4	5
My weight	1	2	3	4	5
My home country	1	2	3	4	5
My health	1	2	3	4	5
My income	1	2	3	4	5

Discuss with a partner.

1. Choose one item that you and your partner rated very differently and one that you rated similarly. Why did you each rate them as you did?

2. In general, what aspects of your life do you consider the most private? Give some examples. Why do you believe in keeping these things to yourself?

3. What factors affect a person's sense of privacy? For example, what roles do culture and personality play?

LISTENING

Preparing to Listen

You are about to listen to a conversation about the privacy of human thoughts and feelings. Answer the questions before you listen. Discuss your answers as a class.

1. What would happen if you could "read" another person's inner thoughts and feelings? How might this be helpful? How might this cause harm?

2. Certain new technologies are being used to discover, or detect, people's emotions. How could these technologies be useful? How could they be dangerous, particularly to a person's sense of privacy?

Listening for Details

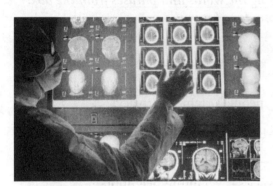
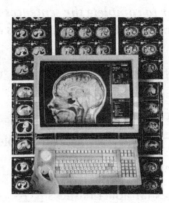

Look over the incomplete statements. Then listen to the conversation at least twice. As you listen, circle the letter of the best answer to complete the sentences. The first one has been done for you.

1. The woman is reading an article about _____.
   a. MRIs
   b. science
   c. news

2. MRI means _____.
   a. magnetic resonance items
   b. magnetic resonance imaging
   c. metallic resonance imaging

3. MRIs show a picture of _____.
   a. the outside of the body
   b. the inside of the body
   c. the brain only

4. New MRIs can help scientists _____.
   a. see what you are feeling
   b. see what you are thinking
   c. see what you know

5. New MRIs can be used to _____.
   a. prove that someone is a criminal
   b. see whether a criminal has violent impulses
   c. catch someone planning a crime

Responding to the Listening

Discuss the questions in small groups.

1. If you could use an MRI to read someone's feelings, whose would you read? Why?

2. Should certain people, such as psychologists, judges, or prison guards, be allowed to use the new MRIs on people without their permission? Why? Should any other group of people be able to use the new MRIs? Who? Why?

3. In what ways could the new MRIs affect people's ability to protect their privacy in the workplace? What could people do in order to defend themselves?

WORDS AND PHRASES ABOUT PRIVACY

Work with a partner to complete the sentences using the words and phrases from the box. Use a dictionary if necessary. The first one has been done for you.

classified	confidential	eavesdrop	~~infringe on~~	intimacy	reluctant

1. Do surveillance cameras ___*infringe on*___ people's right to privacy?

2. Is it right to __eaves·drop__ on people's phone conversations?

3. Some people are extremely __reluctant__ to reveal their age.

4. Building houses far apart reduces __intimacy__ among neighbors.

5. What a patient says to a psychologist is strictly __confidential__.

6. The __classified__ document contained top secret military plans.

Work with a partner. Match the idioms on the left with their definitions on the right. Write the letter on the line. Use a dictionary if necessary. The first one has been done for you.

__c__ 1. behind closed doors

__e__ 2. hush-hush

__d__ 3. invasion of privacy

__b__ 4. keep it to yourself

____ 5. none of your business

a. something you should not be involved in or ask about

b. to not say anything in order to avoid complaining, telling a secret, or causing problems

c. in a place where no one can see you or find out what you are doing

d. a situation in which someone tries to find out personal details about another person's private affairs in a way that is upsetting and often illegal

e. very secret

Work with a partner. Use the words and phrases about privacy to complete the conversation. You might have to change a word's form. When you are done, practice reading aloud the dialogue with your partner. The first one has been done for you.

1. **A:** I think the new MRIs are interesting and can be useful, but I do think they can _____infringe on_____ my privacy; people can see what I am feeling!

   B: Yes. Sharing feelings develops a sense of _____intimacy_____ because you know a lot about the person; you don't do that with just anyone!

2. **A:** Right. I want to choose the people I'm close to!

   B: I would feel hesitant or _____ to have one of those new MRIs if I did not know exactly what it would be used for.

3. **A:** I think my news is _____. If I want people to know, I will tell them myself.

   B: If someone asks me something personal, I could just say it's "_____."

4. **A:** Usually when I tell someone something personal, I follow up by saying "_____," meaning I don't want anyone else to know.

   B: When you stop to think about it, if someone knows my thoughts, reactions, or feelings, it's just like _____eavesdrop_____ on a private conversation.

5. **A:** Yes. And I worry about the way companies and websites collect a lot of personal information about us.

   B: Are those discussions public or are they happening "_____"?

6. **A:** I'm not sure, but the discussions certainly should not be so "_____"; we have a right to know what's going on.

   B: Yes, we do. I understand some information might be _____ because companies don't like to share their information.

7. **A:** Well, we have to be sure our privacy is protected and that no one is looking at our private information without our permission.

   B: Yes, no one should be subject to this kind of _____.

PROBLEM SOLVING

Read and listen to each problem. Then look at the possible solutions given and add one or two of your own. Decide what you would do in each case. Write the reasons for your decision.

Problem 1

A few months ago, you purchased some vitamins online. Now you are receiving a lot of mail, e-mail, and phone calls from businesses trying to sell you vitamins and other health-related products. You find out that the company you bought the vitamins from has sold your personal information to many other companies. Now many companies are advertising to you without your permission. What do you do?

1. Respond to the e-mails, junk mail, and phone calls, demanding that the companies remove you from their lists.

2. Do nothing and use this unsolicited advertising to find out about various health-related products.

3. _____

4. _____

Reasons: _____

_____

Problem 2

Lately, more and more businesses and public spaces in your community have video surveillance cameras that observe and record what people do. City officials and local business owners claim that the surveillance cameras reduce crime, but it's also true that they invade people's privacy. Recently, you decided to skip work and go to the mall with a friend. You called in sick. It just so happened that a video from a surveillance camera was shown on the local news that night and your boss happened to see you. If not for the camera, she would never have learned about your day at the mall. What do you do?

1. Admit to your boss that you lied, but emphasize that the surveillance cameras infringed on your privacy.

2. Go to the owner of the video camera and ask why you were not contacted for permission before the footage was shown.

3. _____

4. _____

Reasons: _____

_____

Your employer allows you and your coworkers to use the computer at work to check your personal e-mail and use the Internet during off hours. However, the employer has also stated that it has the right to inspect your computer activity at any time without obtaining your permission. Recently, a coworker was terminated because she had visited a website that your employer thinks is inappropriate. The employer's explanation was that "some websites are inappropriate in a place of employment, even on the employee's own time." Several of the employees think that this is unfair. What do you do?

1. Request that the employer change the policy. Choosing which websites to view is your own business.

2. Ask the employer to list the types of websites that are forbidden and avoid those sites.

3. _____

4. _____

Reasons: _____

_____

Work in small groups. Talk about each of the previous problems and decide what your group would do. Try to use some of the words and phrases about privacy on page 4.

FROM THE NEWS

Preparing to Read

Answer the questions before you read. Discuss your answers as a class.

1. Have you ever used EZ Pass or another electronic device that is capable of following, or tracking, your movements? If so, describe how the device works.

2. In what situations might it be helpful to trace a person's movements?

3. In what situations might tracing a person's movements be viewed as an invasion of privacy?

Someone Could Be Tracking Your Every Move!

Imagine this. You buy a book, take it home, get in bed to read it, but the store that sold the book can **instantly** find out where you live! How could this be? Well, soon, all that information will be available through Radio Frequency ID tags, or RFIDs. They are very small: as small as a grain of rice. Because of their tiny size, they can be placed in almost everything without our knowing it—even in food!

Some RFIDs are already being used. In the United States, for example, pet owners can get their dog or cat "chipped"—this means **inserting** a special tag under the animal's skin that will allow it to be **identified** by **scanner** if it is lost or stolen. You can also purchase a special tag that allows you to zip on through a tollbooth or get fuel without stopping to pay.

RFIDs in **consumer** items will use something called EPC, or electronic product code. Most people have seen UPCs (universal product codes), or bar codes, on products. EPCs, however, are much different. A UPC can be used to identify **categories** of items—for example, every book of a certain **edition** can have the same UPC. This allows retailers to keep an eye on the sales of a particular book. But, they cannot use the UPC to see the difference between one book and another (for example, the book you bought and the book still on the shelf).

With RFID technology, there will be enough numbers to **track** every individual book. And every individual tire. And every individual pair of pants. Every single item in the world could, in theory, get its own number that would allow it to be tracked no matter where it goes.

There are benefits to this technology: A store owner has information at her fingertips about what's in stock or when certain items are too old and need to be removed or sold on sale. RFIDs could also help with product safety. Your refrigerator could give you a heads up before the milk spoils, or your medicine cabinet might be able to warn you about expired **medication**.

This technological advance could be a benefit to consumers, too. With RFID tags, people may not need to stop and pay for things anymore—if you have an account in a particular store, scanners could check what you have as you leave and **automatically** bill you.

But some people are concerned that RFID tags are an invasion of privacy. They worry that the information could be misused. What you buy and where you go would no longer be private. Anyone with an RFID scanner could know every move you make and every single thing you buy. Are you ready for that?

Checking Your Comprehension

Mark the statements as true (T) or false (F) according to the information and opinions in the article. If a statement is false, correct it to make it true. The first one has been done for you.

1. __T__ RFID tags are extremely small, so they could be placed in almost anything.

2. _____ RFID tags have not yet been used in any consumer products.

3. _____ UPCs, or bar codes, are more precise than RFIDs and EPCs.

4. _____ In theory, bar codes could be used to track every item in the world.

5. _____ RFID tags can provide useful information to retailers.

6. _____ Consumers could use RFID tags to fix their refrigerators and purchase medication.

Thinking Critically About the Reading

Discuss the questions in small groups. Then share your responses with the class.

1. How might RFID tags be a benefit to society? How might they hurt society? Give examples of situations in which these tags could be used positively and negatively.

2. Is tracking of consumer goods a good idea or is it an invasion of people's privacy? Explain your reasoning.

3. If RFID tags are used, who should regulate their use? What sort of restrictions should be in place? For example, should consumers be able to remove them? Why?

4. Think of some examples of RFID tags in your experience. Where have you seen them?

WORDS AND PHRASES FROM THE READING

Look at the words below. Find them in boldface print in the news article on page 8. Look at the context of each word. Can you figure out the meaning? Match the words on the left with their meanings on the right. Use a dictionary if necessary. The first one has been done for you.

___f___ **1.** automatically

___g___ **2.** categories

___i___ **3.** consumer

___a___ **4.** edition

___g___ **5.** identified

_____ **6.** inserting

___e___ **7.** instantly

___b___ **8.** medication

___d___ **9.** scanner

___c___ **10.** track

a. the form that a book is printed in at a particular time

b. drugs or medicine given to people who are sick

c. recognized and named someone or something

d. a machine that can read, trace, or make an image of something

e. immediately

f. by itself or without thinking

g. to follow, monitor, or observe the path of someone or something

h. groups of people or things of the same type

i. someone who buys or uses goods and services

j. putting something inside or into something else

Complete the sentences with these phrases from the reading.

at your fingertips	heads up	zip on through

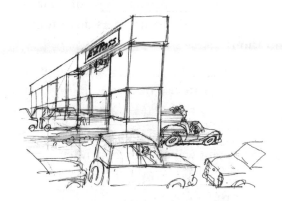

1. Cars can _____ with EZ Pass.

2. This website provides travel information
_____.

3. She's giving her coworker a
_____ about the boss's
bad mood.

Suffixes

Suffixes are word parts added to the end of a word to create a new word. In English, a suffix can be used to change a word's form, or part of speech. Take, for example, the adjective *private*. When you add the suffix *-cy* to *private*, you form the noun *privacy*. Some suffixes such as *-ion, -ience,* and *-ing* can be used to change certain verbs into nouns. For example, if you add the suffix/*-ification* to the verb *identify,* you will form the noun *identification*.

Read the sentences. Look at the two word forms in parentheses. Determine which form is correct for each blank and write it on the line. The first one has been done for you.

1. Many consumers feel that access to personal data is an ____*invasion*____ of their privacy. Businesses want the data for marketing purposes, but consumers don't want their privacy ____*invaded.*____ (invaded/invasion)

2. Modern technology makes it possible for retailers to ____track____ the sale of goods. While this can be beneficial, _____ can also be abused. (track/tracking)

3. Consumers should have the right to _____ access to their personal information. These _____ are an important way to protect privacy. (restrictions/restrict)

4. It's hard to argue against the _____ of RFID tags. It's very _____ to go through a tollbooth on the highway without stopping. (convenient/convenience)

5. Most people have some _____ of privacy in public places. No one _____ to have his or her actions and conversations recorded. (expectation/expects)

CONVERSATION TIP

Knowing the right words and phrases to express what you mean can make conversations go more smoothly. Here are some phrases that will help you express your enthusiasm, persuade someone to go along with you, and accept or decline someone else's idea.

USING ENTHUSIASM TO PERSUADE	
I've got a fantastic idea . . .	
I think it'd be a great idea to . . .	
Doesn't this sound good?	
What do you think about . . .	
Why don't we . . .	
I'm almost certain you'll go along with me on this . . .	

RESPONDING TO SOMEONE ELSE'S IDEA	
Declining	*Accepting*
That sounds good, but I don't think so.	Sure, that sounds great.
I really don't think so because . . .	I'd love to.
No thanks, I'd rather not.	Count me in!
I don't know . . .	Why not!

ACT IT OUT

Act out the situation with a partner. Use the conversation tip expressions in the box and the words and phrases from the unit to act out the following role play.

Situation

You and your partner are new roommates and you want to share a phone line. You must decide whether to get an unlisted phone number. If you get an unlisted phone number, it will not be printed in the telephone book and no one will be able to get it by calling Directory Assistance.

Student A: You like the idea of an unlisted phone number. You have concerns about unwanted calls and think this will help protect your privacy. Try to persuade your partner to get the unlisted phone number. Give at least three reasons why you should get an unlisted number.

Student B: You think an unlisted phone number is not a good idea and don't want to spend the extra money for it. You want your number to be listed so that people can always reach you. Decline your partner's suggestion at least three times before accepting.

> *Student A:* What do you think about getting an unlisted phone number? That means that we can decide who has our phone number and who doesn't.

> *Student B:* I don't know. Maybe someone who didn't have our number would have to reach us in an emergency. Then what would happen?

SAYINGS ABOUT PRIVACY

What do famous actors and other people in the limelight have to say about privacy? Read and discuss the meaning of each quotation in small groups.

◆ *A career is born in public—talent in privacy.*

—Marilyn Monroe
(American actress, 1926–1962)

◆ *I've never looked through a keyhole without finding someone was looking back.*

—Judy Garland
(American actress, 1922–1969)

◆ *The closing of a door can bring blessed privacy and comfort—the opening, terror. Conversely, the closing of a door can be a sad and final thing—the opening a wonderfully joyous moment.*

—Andy Rooney
(American commentator,
producer, author, b. 1919)

◆ *Privacy is not something that I'm merely entitled to, it's an absolute prerequisite.**

—Marlon Brando
(American actor, 1924–2004)

*prerequisite: something that is necessary before something else can happen or be done

Discuss why movie stars often complain about their lack of privacy. Should well-known stars be able to keep their private lives private? Why or why not? How would a famous actor's view of privacy differ from yours? Would you be willing to sacrifice some of your privacy in exchange for fame or great wealth? Why?

BEYOND THE CLASSROOM

People have a mixed response to the topic of privacy. Some people feel personal privacy should be protected at all costs, while others feel there is a need for some kinds of information to be available. Write a short essay about your own views about privacy and privacy protections. Answer questions such as the following:

- Why do you think people have such strong feelings about protecting personal information?

- What kinds of personal information should be protected and why?

- What are the pros and cons of protecting personal information?

- Under what circumstances should personal information be readily available? When should such information remain secret? Explain your reasoning.

Share your ideas in a class discussion.

Is Winning Everything?

THINKING ABOUT THE TOPIC

Talk in small groups or with the whole class.

1. How important is winning to you? Do you agree with the saying: *It's not whether you win or lose, but how you play the game?*

2. What are some right and wrong ways to play sports?

3. In your view, do most professional athletes play by the rules? Explain.

TALKING ABOUT YOUR EXPERIENCE

Most athletes are constantly striving to improve their ability in their particular sport. They want to be the best they can for the sake of the sport and the love of the game. Sometimes the desire to win leads sports stars to do things that other people consider to be ethically wrong. Take the issue of performance-enhancing drugs, for example. Recent news reports have revealed that some highly esteemed athletes have been taking drugs to improve their overall performance.

Take a class survey about the use of performance-enhancing drugs. Answer the survey on your own. When everyone is done, tally the class results by having one student write on the board the number of students who agree and disagree with each statement.

Athletes Caught Using Enhancers . . .	Agree	Disagree
Should be banned from that particular game or event.		
Should be banned from that particular sport or sports event forever.		
Should be stripped of any medals they ever won.		
Should no longer be given credit for any records they set.		
Should be removed from the "Hall of Fame."		

Discuss your responses to the survey with a partner.

1. How were your responses to the survey similar? How were they different? Discuss one point on which you disagreed. Try to explain your reasoning to your partner.

2. Do you think most athletes would respond to this survey the way you did? Why? Would professional athletes have a different response than college or high school athletes? Why?

3. Why do you think that performance-enhancing drugs have become such a problem in professional sports today?

LISTENING

Preparing to Listen

You are about to listen to a conversation between a runner and her coach. Answer the questions before you listen. Discuss your answers as a class.

1. Why might an athlete consider taking performance-enhancing drugs?

2. In your opinion, are there any good reasons for taking performance-enhancing drugs? Explain.

Listening for Details

Look over the questions. Then listen to the conversation at least twice. As you listen, write down your answers to the questions. You do not need to write complete sentences. Just take notes.

1. What is the athlete's complaint?

    _____ Others take _____

2. How does the coach respond?

    _____

3. How is the athlete doing now, compared to six months ago?

    _____

4. What does the athlete say about her times now?

    _____ little better _____

5. What does the athlete want to do?

    _____ take drugs _____

6. Does the coach agree?

    _____ No _____

7. How did the drug help her friend?

    _____ faster & aches, pains _____

8. How does the coach respond?

    _____ No pain no gaine _____

9. What is the most important thing to the athlete?

    _____ being faster. (win) _____

10. What does the athlete say about other runners?

    _____ not fair others take _____

Responding to the Listening

Discuss the questions in small groups.

1. How do you respond to someone who says, "It's not fair. I know other athletes who are taking the drugs"?

2. This athlete is concerned about winning at the expense of her health. What do you think about her attitude? Is winning that important? Why?

WORDS AND PHRASES ABOUT SPORTS

Work with a partner to complete the sentences using the words from the box. Use a dictionary if necessary.

championship	dedication	gifted	sacrifice	stamina	triumph

1. Many athletes have exceptional natural talent or ability. They are truly
   ___gifted___ . Others must work harder to achieve the same level of
   performance.

2. Athletes often have to ___sacrifice___ time with their families and their social life
   in order to spend time training for their sport.

3. Our coach has us work hard and put a lot of effort into our game. He says that
   ___dedication___ to a sport is the key to becoming a great athlete.

4. To run a marathon without stopping to rest requires a great deal of physical and
   mental ___stamina___. Imagine the endurance it takes to run for three to four
   hours without stopping to rest or catch your breath!

5. After many months of hard training and many disappointing losses, our team was
   able to ___triumph___ . We finally won!

6. This year I competed in many local races and consistently won. In this year's final
   race, I will be up against the top runners from all over the country. If I win the
   national ___championship___ I'll be the fastest runner in the country.

Read the sentences and choose the best meaning for each underlined phrase. Circle the letter of the best answer. Use a dictionary if necessary. The first one has been done for you.

1. The team lost, but everyone was <u>a good sport</u> and congratulated the winning
   players.
   a. a person who can deal with defeat without being upset
   b. a person who wins and is very happy about it

2. Audrey's time on the last race was barely faster than the next runner's but she did
   <u>win by a narrow margin.</u>
   a. win by a lot
   b. win by a little

3. Everyone agreed that Robert <u>won hands down</u>; the other swimmers were not even
   close.
   a. almost won
   b. won easily

4. When athletes don't use performance-enhancing drugs, <u>the playing field is level</u>;
   no one has an unfair advantage and everyone is competing fairly.
   a. everything is fair
   b. someone has an unfair advantage

Work with a partner. Use the words and phrases about sports to complete the conversation. Student A reads a sentence. Student B reads the next sentence and completes it with a word or phrase. After completing five items, switch roles. When you are done, practice reading aloud the dialogue with your partner.

1. **A:** After losing a game, I always go up to members of the winning team and congratulate them on a great game.

    B: You are a _good sport_ .

2. **A:** Yesterday, I ran five miles without stopping. I was tired but able to continue the whole time.

    B: You must have a lot of _____ stamina.

3. **A:** I get up at 5:00 A.M. every day to swim. I usually swim for two hours before going to work. Then I swim another hour at night.

    B: You have shown a lot of _dedication_ to swimming.

4. **A:** I enjoy reading about athletes who have worked hard to succeed. I think doing sports is about overcoming obstacles and becoming the best athlete you can, which isn't easy.

    B: To finally succeed in a sport is a great _triumph_ .

5. **A:** Often the most exciting baseball games occur when two teams are so evenly matched that the score is tied until the final moments of the game.

    B: When two teams are neck and neck and then one team _win by a narrow margin_, it is very exciting.

6. **A:** Great athletes like Michael Jordan have extraordinary abilities.

    B: These athletes are extremely _talented_ at what they do.

7. **A:** I am impressed when I hear stories about the personal lives of famous athletes. They have to give up a lot of time with family and friends in order to excel.

    B. They have to _sacrifice_ a lot for their careers.

8. **A:** I only enjoy watching sports when I know that the players are using their natural ability and no one has an unfair advantage.

    B: You like it when _everything is fair_

9. **A:** The winning cyclist was so far ahead of everyone else when she crossed the finish line.

    B: The cyclist _won hands down_

10. **A:** I attended a swimming competition last week with swimmers from all across the country. At the swim meet, the nation's top swimmers competed against each other. The fastest swimmers won medals in each event.

    B: You attended the swimming _championship_

PROBLEM SOLVING

Read and listen to each problem. Then look at the possible solutions given and add one or two of your own. Decide what you would do in each case. Write the reasons for your decision.

Problem 1

You play informal football with a group of friends and neighbors. The players meet once a week for a game. The games are supposed to be casual and fun but not too competitive. The players always start by picking teams. You notice that one player is always picked last. That player is obviously upset that he's everyone's last choice. In addition, the other players criticize him behind his back for being a poor player. What do you do?

1. Try privately to help the player practice and improve.

2. Talk with the other players in private and try to encourage them to pick the player sometimes so that he won't feel bad.

3. _____

4. _____

Reasons: _____

_____

Problem 2

Your friend likes to engage in dangerous, extreme sports. She is married and has a family. Her husband is very concerned about her safety and is worried about something happening to her, possibly leaving him alone with a family to raise. He thinks his wife is being selfish by not thinking about her family and doing what she wants to do. He approaches you and says he has tried to talk to his wife (your friend) but she won't listen. What do you do?

1. Convince the husband to try one of the extreme sports too.

2. Talk to your friend about the risks of extreme sports, but don't mention that her husband approached you.

3. _____

4. _____

Reasons: _____

_____

You play doubles in tennis. Twice your partner has said the other team's ball was out when in fact it wasn't. Because of this, you ended up winning the game. You didn't contradict your partner, but when you mentioned it to him after the game, he said, "What are you worrying about? We won, didn't we?" What do you do?

1. Say nothing; after all, it's only a game.

2. Discuss playing by the rules.

3. _____

4. _____

Reasons: _____

_____

Work in small groups. Talk about each of the previous problems and decide what your group would do. Try to use some of the words and phrases about sports on page 17.

FROM THE NEWS

Preparing to Read

Answer the questions before you read. Discuss your answers as a class.

1. Who bears the primary responsibility for stopping the use of performance-enhancing drugs—the athletes themselves, the drug manufacturers, or the government officials who regulate drug use? Why?

2. Do you feel differently about an athlete when you discover that he or she has been using enhancers? Explain.

3. What do you think is the main reason that athletes use performance-enhancing drugs?

Jason Giambi and Barry Bonds—two professional baseball players recently involved in a steroid scandal

Integrity Matters

By Jim Brancher
The Salinas Californian
Wednesday, December 15, 2004

Question: What are baseball superstars like Jason Giambi and Barry Bonds thinking about when they use performance-enhancing drugs? Do "home run" records still have **integrity?**

Response: Money and fame attract many physically gifted athletes. Their integrity is now being **scrutinized** because an increasing number are taking chemical **shortcuts** to exceptional achievement. Greed and glory are turning Major League Baseball, in particular, into a laboratory for **amoral** scientists and money-hungry pharmaceutical firms.

The baseball players association, with its private-club **atmosphere,** has yet to fully address the problem. Meanwhile, fans **clamor** for their superheroes to set new records. Owners wring their hands, unable to properly discipline inappropriate drug use, while simultaneously allowing dollar signs to cloud sound judgment.

Today's ticket buyers demand an exciting show, and the players have gotten the message. The economic realities are clear: Professional athletes have decided it's worth risking **infamy** and poor health to become famous by setting records, legally or illegally. And the adoring fans, with their shortsighted demands for **gratification,** are perfectly willing to sacrifice the lives of these gladiators.[1] Unless or until the playing field is level, without chemical enhancements, many records could become meaningless.

With the latest reports of improper drug use, more officials are willing to weigh in on abuse of performance-enhancing drugs. From the White House to statehouses around the nation, and now to the Congress, the words are clear: Performance-enhancing drug **abuse** is wrong. Let's stop it.

When will our culture learn this truth? It should be common knowledge that free markets, including baseball players and their respective [2] organizations, must regulate themselves or governments will. Admirable and honest role models are needed. Certainly, gifted athletes are visible and powerful examples. Our society needs visible adults to play by **constructive,** self-imposed rules and behave appropriately, because integrity matters.

[1] *gladiators:* strong men who fought other men or animals in a public event in ancient Rome
[2] *respective:* relating or belonging separately to each person or organization that has been mentioned

Checking Your Comprehension

Write your responses to the following items according to the information and opinions in the news article.

1. What attracts gifted athletes to sports?

   _____

2. Why are more and more athletes taking performance-enhancing drugs?

   _____

3. How are the following groups reacting to the problem of performance-enhancing drug usage?

   a. The baseball players association: _____

   b. Owners: _____

4. What have professional athletes decided when it comes to performance-enhancing drugs?

   _____

5. What has the government said about performance-enhancing drugs?

_____

6. As visible role models, how should athletes behave? Why?

_____

Thinking Critically About the Reading

Discuss in small groups. Then share your responses with the class.

1. Should famous athletes try to be examples of positive values and behavior? Why?

2. If an athlete damages his or her health by using performance-enhancing drugs, is this a private issue or a cause for public concern?

3. Should pharmaceutical companies be allowed to produce performance-enhancing drugs at all? Why?

4. What role, if any, do fans play in the performance-enhancing drug controversy? Explain.

WORDS AND PHRASES FROM THE READING

Look at the words in the box. Find them in boldface print in the news article on page 21. Look at the context of each word. Can you figure out the meaning?

Fill in the crossword puzzle using the words in the box. Use a dictionary if necessary. The first one has been done for you.

| abuse | amoral | ~~atmosphere~~ | clamor | constructive |
| gratification | infamy | integrity | scrutinized | shortcuts |

Across

4. the feeling of an event or place

5. examined someone or something very thoroughly and carefully

8. the state of being evil

9. lacking any standards of right and wrong

10. quicker, more direct ways of going somewhere than the usual ones

Down

1. the satisfaction of a desire or need

2. intended to be helpful or likely to produce good results

3. the use of something in a way that it should not be used

6. to demand or complain about something loudly, as part of a group of people

7. the quality of being honest and of always having high moral principles

4. a t m o s p h e r e

Match the words and phrases on the left with their meanings on the right. Use a dictionary if necessary.

1. _____ cloud sound judgment
2. _____ wring your hands
3. _____ free markets
4. _____ self-imposed
5. _____ shortsighted
6. _____ weigh in on

a. economic systems in which prices are not controlled or limited by the government or any other powerful group

b. to add an opinion to a discussion or argument

c. to rub and twist your hands together because you are worried about something

d. not considering the possible effects in the future of something that seems to save money, time, or effort now

e. accepted without pressure from outside forces

f. to make clear judgment difficult, especially by introducing distracting ideas or information

CONVERSATION TIP

At some time you may be asked to lead or participate in a discussion. Here are some words and phrases that can help you introduce a subject or enter a discussion to make a point.

LEADING AND TAKING PART IN DISCUSSIONS	
Leading/Facilitating	*Entering/Participating*
Who would like to begin?	First of all, I'd like to say that . . .
What do you think about . . . ?	I'd like to begin by saying that . . .
Would someone else like to comment on that?	I agree/disagree with that position because . . .
What is your response?	We should also consider the opposing view . . .
Is there another side to the issue?	I'd like to add to what was said so far.
Does someone have another point to make?	I want to take another perspective on . . .

ACT IT OUT

Have a small-group discussion about the positive and negative aspects of playing sports. Work in groups of three to four students. One student plays the role of the discussion leader. The others are active participants in the discussion, and each person must have at least one turn to talk. Before you begin, read the list of ideas and add several ideas of your own to each list.

Positive aspects of playing sports:

Build stamina and strength
Teach "team spirit" and the ability to work together
Encourage excellence
Keep kids out of trouble

_____

_____

_____

Negative aspects of playing sports:

Too much emphasis on winning
Professional athletes receive too much fame and money
Kids spend too much time on sports and not enough on academic subjects and artistic pursuits

_____

_____

_____

EXAMPLE	

Leader/Facilitator: Who would like to begin?

Participant: I'd like to begin by saying sports today is too much about winning. What I like about sports is the excitement and pleasure of the game.

Sayings About Sports

Almost everyone has something to say about sports. Read and discuss the meaning of each quotation as a class.

◆ *Sports is human life in microcosm.**

—Howard Cosell (American sportscaster, 1918–1995)

**microcosm:* a small group, society, etc., that has the same qualities as a much larger one

How is sports a microcosm of life?

◆ *Sports do not build character. They reveal it.*

—Casey Stengel (American baseball hero, 1890–1975)

What does it mean to reveal character, and how do sports do that? Give an example.

◆ *An athlete cannot run with money in his pockets. He must run with hope in his heart and dreams in his head.*

—Emil Zatopek (Czech distance runner, 1922–2000)

What does this quote say about athletes who become famous and wealthy?

◆ *The finish line is sometimes merely the symbol of victory. All sorts of personal triumphs take place before that point, and the outcome of the race may actually be decided long before the end.*

—Laurence Malone (U.S. champion bike racer, b. 1953)

Do you agree? Give examples of personal triumphs that can take place before a victory.

BEYOND THE CLASSROOM

Famous sports figures have the power to influence people, especially young fans who look up to them as role models. Unfortunately, some star athletes behave badly in public or commit illegal acts. Other athletes use their fame to help companies sell products. Write an essay about whether sports figures should be role models. If so, what kind of models should they be? How should they behave in their private lives? Should they use their fame to sell products? Why or why not? Include positive and negative examples of real sports stars in your essay.

Is the Consumer Always Right?

THINKING ABOUT THE TOPIC

Talk in small groups or with the whole class.

1. What is happening in each picture?
2. Which person is downloading something for free? Is this legal? Why?
3. Should either of the activities shown above be free? Why?

TALKING ABOUT YOUR EXPERIENCE

Consumers have different buying habits and beliefs. They think differently about what to purchase, how much they are willing to pay, or whether a product is worth paying for at all. In addition, the Internet and online shopping have changed the way consumer products are bought and sold.

What do you consider before buying a product? Write down the names of three products you recently purchased. If possible, include an item you bought online. Then analyze your consumer patterns and beliefs. What factors were most important to you for each of the three purchases? Put a checkmark next to factors that influenced you. Add more factors to the chart if necessary.

Product 1:_____	Product 2:_____	Product 3:_____
_____ cost	_____ cost	_____ cost
_____ quality	_____ quality	_____ quality
_____ brand name	_____ brand name	_____ brand name
_____ convenience	_____ convenience	_____ convenience
_____	_____	_____
_____	_____	_____

Discuss with a partner.

1. Compare your charts. How were you and your partner's buying patterns and beliefs similar? How were they different?

2. Were the factors that influenced you different for different products? Explain.

3. Did either you or your partner include an item purchased online? Has online shopping influenced your buying habits? If so, how?

4. What are the benefits and risks of shopping online?

5. What do people obtain for free on the Internet?

LISTENING

Preparing to Listen

You are about to listen to a conversation about the ethics of downloading music from the Internet. Answer the questions before you listen. Discuss your answers with the class.

1. Do you think that people should be allowed to reproduce copyrighted material such as books, videotapes, and CDs? Why?

2. Do you know anyone who has downloaded music from the Internet? If so, did the person pay for the music? Why?

3. What kinds of online music stores and subscription sites are available on the Internet? Have you used any of them? If so, how do they work?

Listening for Details

Listen to the conversation at least twice. As you listen, write the arguments each speaker makes to support his or her point of view.

Speaker 1: Consumers Should Have to Pay to Download Music	Speaker 2: Consumers Should *Not* Have to Pay to Download Music
no — Oline store to purches 99¢ 4 the site — Coping Music is ilegale — music are protected by 2 copy right Lows Expansive to Produse Song writer Singer producer markating /aduertiser music an recording inganer cover artist If the 2 artist choss to offer ther music free to get notice, it should be ther choice.	Network free / site about nobody know Sharing music Over 2 internat & copying is not any difference — Over brist — new music in band who dont have recording company behind them Xide down god with out the low with out paying university response I dont think that is fair I dont agree They are making a lot of money & to much control

If u download uncopy music u do not braking the law
recording company sure can
Euryone awaring the law
neat

Responding to the Listening

Discuss the questions in small groups.

1. Is downloading music from the Internet a form of theft? Why?

2. Should the recording industry sue the parents of children who download copyrighted music without paying? Why?

3. Which speaker do you agree with most? Why? If you don't agree with either speaker, what do you think about the subject?

She

WORDS AND PHRASES ABOUT SHOPPING

Work with a partner to complete the sentences using the words and phrases from the box. Use a dictionary if necessary.

economize	extravagant	frugal	know-how	merchandise	squander

wast money or time

Save money

1. Stores have large sales to get rid of last year's ___squander___ and make room for new products.

2. To most people, money is valuable; one should not _____ money but should use it wisely.

3. When you are trying to save money, you have to look at any and all ways to spend less and _____ .

4. Consumers who do research before buying have the _____know-how_____ to make wise purchases.

5. People who are _____frugal_____ like a good sale!

6. Some people buy items because they are particularly expensive, beautiful, or impressive. They buy _____extravagant_____ items.

Work with a partner. Match the idioms on the left with their definitions on the right. Write the letter on the line. Use a dictionary if necessary.

1. __b__ a steal
2. __d__ rip-off
3. __c__ marked down
4. __e__ sell like hotcakes
5. __a__ window shopping

a. just looking; not buying
b. something that is very cheap
c. reduced in price
d. something that is unreasonably expensive
e. sell fast because it is popular

Work with a partner. Use the words and phrases about shopping to complete the conversation. Student A reads a sentence. Student B reads the next sentence and completes it with a word or phrase. After completing five items, switch roles. When you are done, practice reading the conversation aloud with your partner.

1. **A:** My friend just bought a great new shirt. She said it was <u>very inexpensive</u>.

   B: She said it was _____a steal_____.

2. **A:** I like silk shirts, designer shoes, and other kinds of <u>impressive and expensive</u> clothing.

   B: You have _____extravagant_____ taste in clothes.

3. **A:** Some days I'm <u>just looking</u>. <u>I'm not actually shopping</u> for anything.

   B: Some days you are just _____window shopping_____

4. **A:** The best time to buy things is after a big holiday because the prices are <u>reduced</u>.

   B: Yes, after holidays, merchandise is _____marked down_____.

5. **A:** Right now, I must be <u>careful with money</u> because I am saving up to buy a house.

   B: For now, you have to be _____frugal_____.

6. **A:** Sometimes when I go into a store, there are so many <u>products</u> to choose from!

   B: There is often a bewildering amount of _____merchandise_____ in stores.

7. **A:** While I am a student, I have to find ways to <u>spend less and save money</u>.

   B: As a student, you need to _____economize_____.

8. **A:** I enjoy shopping online because I can research the best products and compare items and prices. I have the <u>skill and practical knowledge</u> I need to shop wisely.

   B: You have the _____know-how_____ to research and buy exactly what you want.

9. **A:** Popular novels like the *Harry Potter* series <u>sell a lot</u>.

   B: Yes, the *Harry Potter* books tend to <u>sell like hotcakes.</u>

10. **A:** I'm an educated consumer and I don't like to <u>waste</u> my money.

    B: You don't like to <u>squander</u> money on foolish purchases.

PROBLEM SOLVING

Read and listen to each problem. Then look at the possible solutions given and add one or two of your own. Decide what you would do in each case. Write the reasons for your decision.

Problem 1

You work for a company that manufactures a product. A friend of yours is in charge of buying supplies for a large company and asks your advice on purchasing the product your company makes. You happen to think a competitor makes a better product than your company does, but you know your company needs the business. Also, you would like to get credit for bringing in the business. What do you do?

1. Be frank about the drawbacks of your company's product, and let your friend decide where to purchase it.

2. Tell your friend to purchase the product from your company.

3. _____

4. _____

Reasons: _____

_____

Problem 2

You are going to a formal affair but don't have enough money to buy an appropriate outfit. A friend suggests that you buy something extravagant, wear it to the event, and return it to the store afterwards. What do you do?

1. Follow your friend's advice.

2. Wear something you already own even though it's not formal enough.

3. _____

4. _____

Reasons: _____

_____

P r o b l e m 3

A TV commercial producer approaches you and a friend. She asks whether you'd like to appear in a commercial with a very famous celebrity. When she tells you the person's name, you can't resist. It is someone you have always wanted to meet. The producer says all you have to do is look very excited about the product and say how great it is. Then she tells you what product the commercial will be advertising. You do not like the product. In fact, you think that it's poorly made and overpriced. It's an item you would never buy yourself because you think it's a rip-off. What do you do?

1. Agree to do the commercial and take advantage of your chance to meet the celebrity.

2. Decline the offer.

3. _____

4. _____

Reasons: _____

_____

Work in small groups. Talk about each of the previous problems and decide what your group would do. Try to use some of the words and phrases about shopping on page 29.

FROM THE NEWS

Preparing to Read

Answer the questions before you read. Discuss your answers as a class.

1. What is your initial reaction when you see a sign selling "two for one" or "buy one get the second one half-price"?

2. Have you ever bought something just because it was on sale, and later wished you hadn't? Describe the situation and your feelings about it.

Buying More: Why Numerical Signs Make You Overspend at the Grocery Store

CHAMPAIGN, IL.—Numerical signs, such as "2 for $2" or "Limit 12 per person" make you spend twice as much as you planned.

Recent studies **conducted** by researchers at the Food and Brand Lab at the University of Illinois found that certain **promotions** have great **effect** on the number of goods purchased. The four studies **spanned** 89 supermarkets and thousands of consumers. The findings were recently **published** in the Journal of Marketing Research.

The research **indicates** that promotions that utilized multi-unit pricing ("3 for $3"), purchase limits ("Limit 12/person"), and suggestive selling[*] ("Buy 10 for your freezer") all doubled the amount consumers purchased—and such promotions can be found throughout grocery stores across the country.

When most people buy products, they buy one or two at a time. They decide on a low number (like one or two), then buy more if the product's on sale. When promotions suggest high numbers ("Buy 12 so you don't run out!"), people shift their reference point to the higher number, and buy more.

"All three types of promotions **increase** purchase amounts from 30% to 105% of what the consumer would **normally** plan on buying," said Dr. Brian Wansink, director of the Food and Brand Lab at the University of Illinois. "But, consumers can **counteract** these promotions. They can write their purchase amounts on their shopping lists and stick to them."

Wansink said that consumers should always be aware of what is really being offered and he offered some "words of wisdom" to consumers.

- Be aware of what the advertisements and **deals** really mean for you, know how much you're actually saving and remember that smaller numbers don't always mean a better deal—but neither do the big numbers.

- Lower limits (two per visit) make consumers buy the product more often while high limits (12 per person) increase the amount of the sale for that visit.

- Suggestive selling (Grab six for studying) is not a sale. It's just a way of promoting the product.

Wansink said the more aware consumers are, the less likely they are to find themselves with a cabinet full of unneeded and unwanted products.

[*] *suggestive selling*: advertising that makes you think a certain way or leads you to believe you are getting a good deal

Checking Your Comprehension

Write your responses to the following items according to the information and opinions in the news article.

1. What is the topic of the article?

   Buying More: Why numerical signs make you overspend at the grocery store

2. Name three kinds of promotions that grocery stores use to increase sales.

   a. _multi-unit pricing ("3 for $3")_

   b. _purchase limits ("limit 12 %")_

   c. _suggestive selling (buy 10 for your freezer)_

3. What can consumers do to resist these types of promotions?

   Be aware of what the advertisements & deals really mean

4. What effect do lower limits, such as "2 for $2" have on consumers?

   decide on a low # then buy more

5. What effect do higher limits, such as "12 per person" have on consumers?

   Shift their reference point to the higher #

Thinking Critically About the Reading

Discuss with a partner. Then share your responses with the class.

1. Have you ever been fooled by an advertisement into buying something you didn't really want or need? Describe the experience. At what point did you realize your mistake? How did you feel?

2. Who is ultimately responsible for knowing a good deal—the consumer or the seller? Why?

3. Why do you think consumers are so easily convinced to buy more than they need?

WORDS AND PHRASES FROM THE READING

Look at the words below. Find them in boldface print in the news article on page 33. Look at the context of each word. Can you figure out the meaning? Match the words on the left with their meanings on the right. Use a dictionary if necessary.

1. __i__ conducted
2. _____ counteract
3. __c__ deals
4. __d__ effect
5. __b__ increase
6. __g__ indicates
7. __e__ normally
8. __a__ promotions
9. __j__ published
10. _____ spanned

a. activities intended to help sell a product

b. become larger in amount or degree

c. agreements or arrangements, especially in business, such as good prices

d. the way a person, action or event changes someone or something

e. shows that a particular situation exists

f. usually, under typical conditions

g. printed in a book, newspaper, journal, etc.

h. reduce or prevent the bad effect of something by doing something that has the opposite effect

i. did something to get information or prove facts

j. included all of a particular space, area, or time

Complete the paragraph with these phrases from the reading.

reference point	stick to them	words of wisdom

This article offers some (1) _words of wisdom_ to people who want to be informed consumers. Before you go shopping, know exactly what you want to buy and how much of each item you really need. Put your purchase amounts on your shopping list, and (2) _stick to them_. Then you will have a clear (3) _reference point_ for making purchases and won't be swayed by store promotions to buy things you don't want or need.

Conversation Tip

When you enter a store, a salesperson may give you a "sales pitch"—saying things to persuade you to buy something. Suppose you are not interested or only want to go window shopping. Here are some ways to interrupt politely and say "no."

Saying "No" to a Salesperson	
Formal	Excuse me, but no thank you. I beg your pardon, but I am not looking for . . . I appreciate your help, but no. No, thank you. I'm just looking/browsing/window shopping.
Informal	Thanks, but I'm really not interested. Not today, but thanks anyway.

Act It Out

Act out the situation with a partner. Use the expressions in the conversation tip box and the words and phrases from the unit to act out the following role play.

Situation

Student A: You are a salesperson who gets a commission (a fee) for each item you sell. Your goal is to sell as much merchandise as possible. You must try to convince shoppers to buy your store's products. Each time a shopper says no, you need to point out why the deal is good or talk about another product the customer might want to buy.

Student B: You are a frugal shopper in search of the best deal. Your goal is to save money and not be taken in by sales schemes or fast-talking sales people. You must say no to the salesperson at least three times.

> **EXAMPLE**
>
> **Salesperson:** *Hi. Can I help you find something?*
>
> **Customer:** *No, thank you. I'm just window shopping.*
>
> **Salesperson:** *Well, we have some incredible deals today. Take our book bags for example. Buy one, and you get a second one at half-price. And they are available in a variety of colors. Let me show you.*
>
> **Customer:** *Thanks, but I'm really not interested.*
>
> **Salesperson:** *Can I help you find something else? Maybe a wallet? These wallets have been selling like hotcakes.*
>
> **Customer:** *Not today, but thanks anyway.*

Sayings About Buying and Selling Products

What do people have to say about shopping? Read and discuss the meaning of each quotation as a class. Which quotes do you agree with, and why?

◆ *Caveat emptor ("Buyer beware")*

—Anonymous, from ancient Rome

◆ *There's a sucker born every minute.*

—David Hannum
(American banker and horse trader, 1832–1892)

◆ *The odds of going to the store for a loaf of bread and coming out with ONLY a loaf of bread are three billion to one.*

—Erma Bombeck (American writer and humorist, 1927–1996)

◆ *A business that makes nothing but money is a poor kind of business.*

—Henry Ford (American founder of Ford
Motor Company, 1863–1947)

◆ *Whenever you see a successful business, someone once made a courageous decision.*

—Peter F. Drucker (Austrian-born writer, management
consultant, and professor, b. 1909)

Think of an example in which one of the sayings applies. It can be an experience you have had or a situation you know about. Share it with the class.

Beyond the Classroom

In this unit you explored the ethics of suggestive selling. Analyze your own views about advertising and consumer rights. Select an advertisement that you have seen online, on TV, or in a newspaper or magazine. Pick one that you feel strongly about—because you either like it or find it offensive. Write a detailed description of the advertisement. Answer questions like the following:

• How does the ad try to appeal to consumers?

• In what ways is the ad effective or ineffective?

• Is the ad suggestive or deceptive in some ways? If so, how does the ad mislead consumers?

• Could the ad provide more information? Would this make the product or service more attractive or less so? Why?

Bring in a copy of the ad if possible and share your thoughts about it with the class.

UNIT 4

Why Blow the Whistle?

THINKING ABOUT THE TOPIC

Talk in small groups or with the whole class.

1. Which cartoon shows a tattletale—someone who tells a parent or teacher that another child has done something bad?

2. Which cartoon shows a possible whistle-blower—someone who tells people in authority about dishonest or illegal practices?

3. Why does a child tattle?

4. Why does a person blow the whistle?

5. Why do some people respect a whistle-blower, while others hate that person?

TALKING ABOUT YOUR EXPERIENCE

Whistle-blowers are willing to come forward and expose wrongdoing when others might say nothing. Often they are fired for exposing misconduct and find it difficult to obtain employment elsewhere.

When would you report misconduct because of your sense of right and wrong?
Read the situations in the chart below. How would you react? Check your responses.

Situation	I Wouldn't Say Anything	I Might Say Something	I Would Definitely Say Something
1. You found out that the factory where you are employed is secretly releasing dangerous gases into the air.			
2. You discovered that an Internet company has been overcharging customers on their bills. You are both an employee and a customer of the company.			
3. You work for a drug manufacturer and know that the company has released a new drug without testing it properly. This drug could cause severe health problems.			

Discuss with a partner.

1. How were your responses similar and different? Talk about one situation in which you responded differently.

2. What factors did you consider before you responded to each situation?

3. What effect might your responses have on your job, your coworkers, the company, your family, or the general public? Which effects might be positive? Which might be negative?

LISTENING

Preparing to Listen

You are about to listen to a conversation between a potential whistle-blower and his close friend. Answer the questions before you listen.

1. Why do people become whistle-blowers?

2. In what ways do whistle-blowers suffer or gain as a result of their actions?

3. Why do honest people keep quiet when a company or a government is doing something wrong?

Listening for Details

There are steps to consider before blowing the whistle. Read the five steps below. Listen to the conversation at least twice. As you listen, number the steps from 1 to 5 as they are presented in the listening. The first one has been done for you. When you are finished, compare your answers with a partner's. If necessary, listen to the conversation again.

Steps to Consider Before Blowing the Whistle

___1___ Try to talk to management to resolve the problem.

_____ Include your family in the decision. How does your family feel about you blowing the whistle?

_____ Hire a good attorney to help you determine if you have a good case.

_____ Ask yourself if you are willing to risk what might happen to you.

_____ Ask yourself if the wrongdoing is severe enough for you to report.

Responding to the Listening

Discuss the questions in small groups.

1. Do you think the man should blow the whistle? Why?

2. If the man decides to blow the whistle, what may happen to him and his family?

3. What might happen if the man decides not to say anything?

4. What advice would you give the man? Be specific.

5. Would you blow the whistle in this situation? Why or why not?

WORDS AND PHRASES ABOUT WHISTLE-BLOWERS

Work with a partner to complete the sentences using the words from the box. Use a dictionary if necessary.

anonymous	conscientious	consequences	informers	misconduct

1. Many whistle-blowers are extremely _____ people who show the same kind of care and attention in their private lives that they do at work.

2. Most whistle-blowers expose wrongdoing because of moral principles, not in order to make money. In this way they are unlike _____, who expose misconduct for personal gain.

3. Once a whistle-blower's identity is known, the person can no longer remain _____.

4. Whistle-blowers suffer a variety of negative _____ as a result of their actions; they may be demoted or fired or receive threats.

5. The company was accused of various types of financial _____, including misrepresenting its profits and losses.

Work with a partner. Match the informal expressions on the left with their definitions on the right. Write the letter on the line. Use a dictionary if necessary.

1. _____ fall guy
2. _____ to let the cat out of the bag
3. _____ to get the ax
4. _____ to name names
5. _____ to rat on
6. _____ to take the rap

a. to be blamed or punished for a mistake or a crime, especially unfairly

b. to reveal the identities of people who are involved in something, especially something wrong or something they want to hide

c. to be disloyal to someone, especially by telling someone in authority about something wrong that person has done

d. to tell a secret, especially without intending to

e. someone who is punished for someone else's crime

f. to be dismissed from your job

PROBLEM SOLVING

Read and listen to each problem. Then look at the possible solutions and add one or two of your own. Decide what you would do in each case. Write the reasons for your decision.

Problem 1

Your company has a government contract to build pipes. You know that the pipes are not of good quality and will cause environmental problems in five years. You don't plan to be working at the company or living in the area for very long. What do you do?

1. You tell your supervisor about the potential problems.

2. You leave the problem for another employee to take care of.

3. _____

4. _____

Reasons: _____

_____

Problem 2

Your company throws away old computers. A coworker takes those computers and sells them on eBay. Another coworker tells the boss. The first person loses his job. The informer is promoted. How do you feel about the informer? Why?

1. You think the informer did the right thing.

2. You think the informer should not have said anything.

3. _____

4. _____

Reasons: _____

_____

Problem 3

You work for a medical equipment manufacturer. You notice a serious design flaw in one of the company's life-support machines. Fixing the problem would be easy and inexpensive but the possible consequences of not fixing it could kill. You tell your supervisor. When she does not respond, you call the government agency that oversees your company. The next day you are fired. What do you do?

1. You start filing a whistle-blower case.

2. You approach your boss to discuss your firing.

3. _____

4. _____

Reasons: _____

_____

Work in small groups. Talk about each of the previous problems and decide what your group would do. Try to use some of the phrases about whistle-blowers on page 40.

Preparing to Read

Answer the questions before you read. Discuss your answers as a class.

1. Have you read or heard about any famous whistle-blowing cases recently in the news? If so, describe one of the cases.

2. What movies have you seen about real and fictional whistle-blowers? For example, have you seen *Silkwood, Erin Brockovich,* or *The Insider*?

3. What are some of the worst consequences of whistle-blowing?

Whistle-Blowers' Concern About Retaliation Justified

Sherron Watkins had good reason, or is **justified,** to be concerned that she might suffer **retaliation** for **exposing** the accounting **scandal** at Enron, according to Joyce Rothschild, who has conducted the only national study of whistle-blowers from all types of jobs.

Rothschild, professor of sociology at Virginia Tech, did an eight-year study of in-depth interviews with 300 whistle-blowers and more than 200 surveys of silent observers (people who observed wrongdoing but remained silent). She found that 69 percent were fired as a result of exposing wrongdoing, even when they only reported this wrongdoing to their supervisors. Of those who reported **unethical** or illegal behavior to outside **authorities,** Rothschild found that over 80 percent were fired.

Rothschild, who has published five academic articles on her studies, found in many cases that the moment senior management realized that an individual might blow the whistle, they began a race to show the would-be whistle-blower was wrong or not to be believed before the whistle-blower could reveal the management's unethical behavior. The whistle-blowers were almost always affected. In 84 percent of her cases, former whistle-blowers said they became depressed and could no longer trust the managers of organizations. In 53 percent of the cases, whistle-blowers suffered **deterioration** even in their family relations.

Statistical analysis of the data determined that the greater and more widespread the observed misconduct reported by the whistle-blower, the more swift and severe the **reprisals.** Gender, race, age, educational level, and years on the job did not protect a whistle-blower from retaliation.

So what makes people take these personal risks? Rothschild found that 79 percent of her whistle-blowers acted because of their values. According to Rothschild, some whistle-blowers said that they got their sense of right and wrong from the codes of professional ethics of their various occupations; some said their moral compass was a result of religious upbringing or family teaching; but in nearly all cases, they said they were trying to "do the right thing." Of those who acted for other reasons, 16 percent said that their whistle-blowing was because they were afraid that they would be blamed for the misconduct of others.

Rothschild believes we need more laws to protect whistle-blowers from retaliation so that they can speak honestly to their superiors. Moreover, Rothschild said given the number of organizations in her study whose first response was to get rid of the whistle-blower and to **suppress** whatever critical information they may have had, the evidence suggests strongly that organizations of all types have a long way to go in learning how to **tolerate** and even benefit from whistle-blowers.

Checking Your Comprehension

Write your responses to the following items according to the information and opinions in the news article.

1. What is the main idea of the reading? State it in your own words.

   _____

2. List two details that support the main idea.

   _____

   _____

Scan the article for statistics about whistle-blowers. Then fill in the chart below.

Total number of whistle-blowers and silent observers Rothschild interviewed	
Percentage of people interviewed who were fired because they exposed wrong doing to a manager in the company	
Percentage who were fired for reporting wrongdoing to someone outside the company	
Percentage of those interviewed who became depressed and could no longer trust management	
Percentage whose family relationships suffered	
Percentage who took action because of their value system	
Percentage who said that they were trying to avoid blame for others' misconduct	

Thinking Critically About the Reading

Discuss with a partner. Then share your responses with the class.

1. Do any of the statistics in the chart above surprise you? Why?

2. What kind of misconduct would you be willing to speak up about?

3. Would you be willing to speak up even if you thought you would experience retaliation? Why?

4. How bad would a situation have to be in order for you to risk your job and your family's security? For example, would financial misconduct be enough or would the unethical behavior have to involve health risks to many people?

5. Would you come forward and support a whistle-blower in court if you agreed with what the person had to say? Why or why not?

WORDS AND PHRASES FROM THE READING

Look at the words in the box. Find them in boldface print in the news article on page 42. Look at the context of each word. Can you figure out the meaning?

Read the sentences. Circle the letter of the best definition for each underlined word.

authorities	deterioration	exposing	justified	reprisals
retaliation	scandal	suppress	tolerate	unethical

1. Whistle-blowers are often <u>justified</u> in worrying about their jobs.
   a. having a valid explanation or reason
   b. having a great deal of stress

2. Employees are afraid they will be fired or experience other <u>retaliation</u> if they report what they see.
   a. an action against someone who has done something bad to you
   b. an action done in the hope that it will result in something good later

3. Some whistle-blowers experienced a <u>deterioration</u> in their home life, including more disagreements and increased stress among family members.
   a. the development into a bad situation
   b. the improvement of family problems

4. Often employees go to outside <u>authorities</u> such as the government to help them resolve a case.
   a. a group of employees
   b. the people or organizations that are in charge of a particular country or area

5. Companies might try to <u>suppress</u> evidence of wrongdoing. They do not want to draw attention to their unethical behavior.
   a. to make information known
   b. to prevent important information from becoming known

6. Often management won't <u>tolerate</u> the views of whistle-blowers, so whistle-blowers are often fired.
   a. to criticize people for behaving a certain way or saying something
   b. to allow people to do, say, or believe something without criticizing or punishing them

7. The incident at Enron was a large <u>scandal</u>, one of many recently in large corporations. Enron's improper actions have drawn a lot of media attention.
   a. a behavior or event, often involving famous people, that is considered to be shocking or not moral
   b. an action corporations take while doing business

8. More and more whistle-blowers are <u>exposing</u> wrongdoings. People have a right to know when serious misconduct occurs within a company.
   a. covering up an event that is unacceptable
   b. telling the truth about an event or situation that is unacceptable

9. Many whistle-blowers suffer <u>reprisals</u> for their behavior. Often they lose their jobs and some even receive death threats.
   a. acts of violence or other strong reactions to punish enemies or opponents for something they have done
   b. termination from a job for something the employee has done

10. There is no reason to remain silent about <u>unethical</u> behavior. A strong sense of right and wrong leads many people to report wrongdoing.
    a. morally bad or incorrect
    b. morally good or correct

Match the phrases on the left with their meanings on the right.

1. _____ codes of professional ethics

2. _____ get rid of

3. _____ moral compass

   a. to make someone leave because you do not like them or because they are causing problems

   b. the moral rules related to a specific line of work or occupation

   c. a personal sense of right and wrong that is based on an individual's values

CONVERSATION TIP

When you have to confront a difficult situation, there are phrases you can use to lead into what you have to say. Here are some phrases and sentences you can use to deal tactfully with touchy situations.

CONFRONTING A DIFFICULT SITUATION
We need to talk.
I've got something I need to say.
I am not sure how to say this but . . .
This is really difficult to say.
You may not want to hear this but . . .
I'm sorry but I really need to say this.

ACT IT OUT

Act out the situation. Use the conversation tip expressions in the box and the words and phrases from the unit to act out the following role play.

Situation

You and your colleague have been assigned a timeframe to complete a project. Your colleague hasn't been very cooperative and, most importantly, abuses time. He takes two-hour lunches, is always on the Internet, and makes many personal phone calls. You have done most of the work on the project. You know that he really needs some type of job, but he is terrible in his current position. If you tell the boss, your colleague will lose his job. You must confront your colleague and tell him how you feel.

Student A: You are the colleague who does all the work.

Student B: You are the colleague who abuses his time.

Student A: *Hi. I've got something I need to say.*

Student B: *Sure, what's the problem?*

Student A: *I'm not sure how to say this, but you haven't been doing your fair share of the work on this project.*

Student B: *Well, I've had some things on my mind lately, but I hope you won't go to the boss about this. If you do, I might get the ax.*

PROVERBS AND SAYINGS ABOUT SPEAKING THE TRUTH

Explore what people have thought and said about speaking up when wrongs are committed. Read and discuss the meaning of each quotation in small groups. Which ones do you agree with? Answer the questions following the quotes.

◆ *He who does not bellow the truth when he knows the truth makes himself the accomplice of liars and forgers.*

—Charles Péguy
(French poet, philosopher, and essayist, 1873–1914)

◆ *He who has approved of wrongdoing is as guilty as he who has committed it.*

—Arabian Proverb

When you don't tell the truth about an unethical situation, are you part of the problem?

◆ *Truth and oil always come to the surface.*

—Spanish Proverb

Does the truth always come out? If so, why? If not, give an example of an instance in which it did not.

◆ *No matter how far down a wrong road you are, turn back.*

—Turkish Proverb

How does this apply to whistle-blowers who come forward after putting up with a situation for a long time?

BEYOND THE CLASSROOM

Watch one of the following movies about a whistle-blower: Silkwood, Erin Brockovich, *or* The Insider. *Afterwards, do some additional research about the actual case. Then write a short report including the following information:*

- What type of person was the whistle-blower? Use adjectives to describe his or her character traits.

- What did the whistle-blower expose?

- What were the consequences of the whistle-blower's actions?

- What did you think about the whistle-blower? Did you agree with the actions?

- What would you have done in the same situation?

Share your reports with the class.

Is *That* Entertainment?

THINKING ABOUT THE TOPIC

Talk in small groups or with the whole class.

1. What type of entertainment is going on in each picture?

2. Which of these events would you find entertaining? Why?

3. Which of these events involves some risk to the participants?

4. In your opinion, does an element of danger make an event more entertaining? Why? Would your opinion change if you knew the people participating in the event?

TALKING ABOUT YOUR EXPERIENCE

When it comes to entertainment, people have widely varied tastes. A particular type, or *genre*, of entertainment may appeal to one person, but not another. People with a good sense of humor might love comedies. People who like excitement might be drawn to thrillers or mysteries.

Use the chart below to assess your own tastes in entertainment. Read the Genre column. How much do you like each type of entertainment? Rate your feelings from 1 to 5, with 1 being "I like it a lot" and 5 being "I don't like it much." Circle the number that best represents your feelings about each genre.

Genre/Type of Entertainment	Like it a Lot ←----------------------→ Don't Like it Much				
Comedy	1	(2)	3	4	5
Romance	1	(2)	3	4	5
Drama	(1)	2	3	4	5
Mysteries/Thrillers	1	2	3	4	5
Celebrity Interviews	(1)	2	3	4	5
Documentaries	1	2	(3)	4	5
News Programs	1	2	(3)	4	5
Science Fiction	1	2	(3)	4	5
Animation	1	2	3	(4)	5
Quiz Shows	1	2	3	(4)	5

Discuss with a partner.

1. Compare your charts. How were you and your partner's tastes in entertainment similar and different?

2. Select one or two of your favorite genres. Tell your partner why you like this type of entertainment. Give examples of specific shows in this genre that you like.

LISTENING

Preparing to Listen

Reality TV is a genre in which there are no actors and no scripts. Real people are placed in dramatic situations while the camera records their reactions. There are a wide variety of reality TV shows—some are similar to soap operas while others are like contests or quiz shows.

You are about to hear an interview with several people about reality TV. Answer the questions as a class before you listen. Discuss your answers with the class.

1. What do you think draws people to reality TV?
2. Why might someone prefer reality TV to a movie, or vice versa?
3. Why do you think producers make reality TV shows?

Listening for Details

Read the names, abbreviations, and statements below. Then listen to the interview at least twice. As you listen, identify the show that each comment is about. Write the initials for the correct show on the line.

B=Big Brother D=Big Diet S=Survivor A=The Apprentice I=American Idol

1. __B__ Public humiliation and rejection
2. __B__ Not compassionate
3. __D__ Should not profit from another's embarrassment or failure
4. __A__ Can learn a lot about business; educational
5. __D__ Motivates a person to improve
6. __I__ Winners feel so good
7. __I__ Winners get a once in a lifetime opportunity
8. __I__ Losers aren't talented, and they need to find out
9. __S__ Like the struggles we face in our own lives
10. __S__ Enjoy watching the skill involved
11. __S__ Like the problem solving and the suspense

Responding to the Listening

Discuss the questions in small groups.

1. How is reality TV different from TV shows about fictional people and situations?
2. Look at the list above, and place a "+" next to the positive reasons for watching and producing reality TV shows. Do you agree with these reasons? Why? In your opinion are reality TV shows a positive or negative form of entertainment? Explain.
3. Who bears the main responsibility for the content of reality TV programs—the producers, the directors, the participants, or the audience? Explain.

WORDS AND PHRASES ABOUT WATCHING OTHERS

Work with a partner to complete the sentences using the words and phrases from the box. Use a dictionary if necessary.

gawk *stare stupidly*	glance *quick look*	rubbernecking *something made of it*	spectator *person who looks on*	voyeuristic

1. It is hard not to _____gawk_____ when you see a famous film star or well-known musician.

2. Some people criticize the _____voyeuristic_____ aspect of reality TV; these programs allow viewers to watch other people's private suffering and embarrassment.

3. I never understood the act of _____rubbernecking_____; why would you want to see someone who just had an accident on the highway?

4. Some people want to participate in reality TV programs; others feel more comfortable playing the role of _____spectator_____.

5. I don't like to stare at people, so sometimes I just _____glance_____ at someone quickly.

Complete the sentences with the phrases below. Use a dictionary if necessary.

can't take their eyes off	catch a glimpse of	getting a kick out of

1. She is _getting a kick out of_ the movie.

2. The fan craned his neck to _catch a glimpse of_ the film star.

3. They just _can't take their eyes off_ each other.

PROBLEM SOLVING

Read and listen to each problem. Then look at the possible solutions given and add some of your own. Decide what you would do in each case. Write the reasons for your decision.

Problem 1

The producers of a new reality TV show are looking for a group of close friends to be the contestants. You have a very close group of friends who want to be on the show. You value your mutual friendships very much. The show involves competing against your best friends. You know that only one of you can win, and the rest must lose. If you were to win, you would receive a lot of money. You like to act and appearing on the show might lead to an acting career in show business. Nevertheless, you are concerned about ruining your friendships. What do you do?

1. Apply and if chosen go on the show and compete with your friends.

2. Decide not to be on the show and find another way to advance your acting career.

3. _____

4. _____

Reasons: _____

_____

Problem 2

A new reality TV show has just come out. You and many people feel the show has gone too far and that the contents are distasteful and offensive. You refuse to watch the show, and you don't think that anyone should be watching or participating in this type of "entertainment." Although you believe strongly in free speech and are opposed to censorship, this seems to be a special case. What do you do?

1. Write letters to the network and producer and publicize your feelings about the show in the media—newspapers, TV, etc.

2. Avoid watching the show and tell your friends and acquaintances not to watch it.

3. _____

4. _____

Reasons: _____

_____

Work in small groups. Talk about each of the previous problems and decide what your group would do. Try to use some of the words and phrases about watching others on page 51.

FROM THE NEWS

Preparing to Read

Answer the questions before you read. Discuss your answers as a class.

1. Why has reality TV become so popular worldwide?
2. Who decides on the content of the shows? How do you think these decisions are made?
3. In what ways might reality TV programs vary from country to country?
4. What sort of reality TV programs would you like to see on the air?

Reality TV*

Viewers worldwide are tuning in to Reality TV
Cable channel content varies from country to country

By Steve Brennan
Hollywood Reporter

LOS ANGELES—Call it morbid curiosity, or, better yet, "rubbernecking." Whatever you call it, it seems to be **endemic** to drivers worldwide. Sad but true, most people tend to slow down and **peer** at accident scenes on the highway.

But what does that have to do with the world of international TV? Well, it's that same attraction to tragedy that has fueled the success of a worldwide channel dedicated mostly to crash-and-burn reality TV.

Launched in December 1999, Reality TV is one of the fastest-growing international channel brands worldwide. In just four years, it has gained distribution in more than 125 territories and **claims** 35 million **subscribers.**

In 2003, Reality TV launched services in India, Latin America, the Philippines, Ireland, and Israel and is currently launching in the United States. It is available throughout Europe, the United Kingdom, Africa, the Middle East, and Asia. In all territories, Reality TV carries a mix of programming, from natural disasters to medical emergencies and everyday **mishaps**. But the man behind the operation stresses that tastes for reality can vary vastly from country to country.

"When we launched in India, we realized that some reality shows would be culturally unacceptable there," says Chris Wronski, chairman and president of London-based Zone Vision, parent company of Reality TV, and the creator of the **enterprise**. "We (reach) 14 million homes in India, so it's an important market for us, and we have to be careful not to offend anybody."

Even within Europe, tastes and **standards** vary, Wronski says. "For example, we have a show from Spain called 'Impacto TV' that gets in close (on accident scenes) and shows more blood than you would normally see. In Central Europe, that's something that is expected, but in the United Kingdom that would not be acceptable."

Wronski stresses that although reality television travels much better than most genres, the success of his company depends on being extremely aware of cultural boundaries when it comes to programming on a worldwide basis. "There is always a lot of discussion before the launch of a channel in order to make sure that we will not offend anybody. But it's also critical to make sure that the programming we do air in a specific market has the greatest possible **appeal**. It takes about a year for us to get ready for each one of the territories that we enter, and of course we always have a local team working in that territory."

Why does Wronski believe that Reality TV is such a favorite of viewers everywhere? "Well somebody once observed that reality is stranger than fiction, and it is. This is true drama, real human beings. But in many cases—such as 'Rescue 911'—it's also about people risking their lives to save people, and that can be **inspiring.** It's not always about accidents on the motorway."

---

*In this article, *Reality TV* (with a capital "R") is the name of a channel devoted to a special kind of reality television programming. The *Reality TV* channel focuses on everything from the heroism of firefighters, police, and medical staff to uplifting accounts of individual bravery. *Reality TV* uses video footage filmed during real-life events and allows viewers to see extraordinary adventures through the eyes of the people who lived them. There are no actors or special effects.

Checking Your Comprehension

Write your responses to the following items according to the information and opinions in the news article.

1. How is the appeal of the Reality TV channel like that of rubbernecking?

   _____

2. How many territories have Reality TV programs, and how many viewers subscribe to the channel worldwide?

   _____

3. Why do producers of Reality TV programs have to be careful before they launch a show in a particular place?

   _____

4. Why wouldn't "Impacto TV" be popular in the United Kingdom?

   _____

5. In what ways are certain Reality TV programs inspiring?

   _____

Thinking Critically About the Reading

Discuss in small groups. Then share your responses with the class.

1. In your opinion, do people find Reality TV programs inspiring or are viewers just attracted to tragedy?

2. The article says, "It takes about a year for us to get ready for each one of the territories that we enter." Why does it take so long to launch a show? What might producers do to prepare to enter a new territory?

3. Should producers of all reality TV shows be culturally sensitive? Why?

WORDS AND PHRASES FROM THE READING

Look at the target words below. Find them in boldfaced print in the news article on page 53. Look at the context of each word. Can you figure out the meaning? Match the words on the left with their meanings on the right. Use a dictionary if necessary.

1. __b__ appeal

2. __ __ claims

3. __a__ endemic

4. __c__ enterprise

5. __h__ inspiring

6. __g__ launched

7. __d__ mishaps

8. __i__ peer

a. always present in a particular place, or among a particular group of people

b. a quality that makes someone or something attractive or interesting to you

c. a company, organization, or business, especially a new one

d. small accidents or mistakes that do not have serious results

e. people who give money regularly for a service

f. ideas of what is good or normal

g. started something new

9. __f__ standards

10. __e__ subscribers

h. giving people energy, a feeling of excitement, and a desire to do something great

i. to look very carefully or hard, especially because you cannot see something well

j. states that something is true even though it has not been proven

Collocations

Collocations are words that commonly occur together. For example, English speakers often use the following word patterns: *stormy weather, commit a crime,* or *fame and fortune.* Collocations occur in different patterns such as adjective + noun, noun + noun, verb + noun, and noun + verb. Study the following examples.

> EXAMPLE
>
> adjective + noun
>
> *Our flight was canceled because of <u>stormy weather</u>.*
>
> noun + noun
>
> *Some people become actors because they are seeking <u>fame and fortune</u>.*
>
> verb + noun
>
> *He went to jail because he <u>committed a crime</u>.*

The following sentences contain collocations from the reading. Read the sentences, and circle the letter of the best meaning for each underlined collocation. Use a dictionary if necessary.

1. Whenever I go to the movies and there is any kind of violence, I have to turn away. My friend loves to see it all! I guess she has a <u>morbid curiosity</u>.
   a. a strong curiosity for disgusting subjects
   b. a curiosity about movies

2. I am always amazed to see newscasters on the scene when <u>natural disasters</u> occur; I saw one woman reporting from the scene of a terrible hurricane and another from a flood. I was worried for their safety.
   a. dangerous newscasts
   b. sudden events, not caused by people, that cause great damage or suffering

3. I saw one reality TV program all about <u>medical emergencies</u>. The camera crew filmed at accident scenes. Viewers could watch injured or sick people being treated by medical teams, which I found distasteful.
   a. unexpected and dangerous situations involving injuries and illness
   b. ambulances rushing to the scene of accidents

4. The more we watch any one genre of entertainment, the more motivation there is for producers to make more of the same. We as viewers <u>fuel the success</u> of programs and movies.
   a. encourage the production and popularity
   b. produce new types

Write your own sentences using each of the collocations above.

1. _____

2. _____

3. _____

4. _____

CONVERSATION TIP

Sometimes you need to express your disapproval for something and let people know that you think it is wrong or in bad taste. Here are some words and phrases that will help you express your disapproval about someone or something. Some of the language is formal and polite, and some of it is informal or slang.

EXPRESSING DISAPPROVAL	
Formal/Polite	*Informal/Slang*
I find this . . .	This is really . . .
objectionable	gross
distasteful	revolting
offensive	foul
too graphic	This turns my stomach
off-putting	sickens me
disgraceful	disgusts me

ACT IT OUT

Work with a partner. Use the conversation tip expressions in the box and the words and phrases from the unit to act out the following role play.

Situation

Student A: You and someone you have just met are watching a new reality TV show. The contestants on the show are doing something you find unbearable to watch. You want to turn off the TV. Express your disapproval to this person whom you barely know, and explain why you feel the way you do.

Student B: You are watching the same show, but are a bit puzzled by Student A's reaction. You have seen the contestants do this sort of thing before and don't mind it. You must ask Student A to explain his/her reaction.

> **EXAMPLE**
>
> **Student A:** *This show is objectionable. I can't watch it another minute.*
>
> **Student B:** *What do you mean?*
>
> **Student A:** *How could the producers ask the contestants to . . .*

Student B: *I guess you don't watch this show often. This is very typical. What bothers you about it?*

Student A: *I find it offensive that they would . . .*

SAYINGS ABOUT ENTERTAINMENT

Sayings About Television

Explore what people have said for and against television. Read and discuss the meaning of each quotation in small groups.

◆ *All television is children's television.*

—Richard P. Adler (American composer and lyricist, b. 1921)

◆ *Television is chewing gum for the eyes.*

—Frank Lloyd Wright (American architect, 1867–1959)

◆ *Television is the first truly democratic culture, the first culture available to everybody and entirely governed by what the people want. The most terrifying thing is what people do want.*

—Clive Barnes (English critic and writer, b. 1927)

◆ *Television is teaching all the time. Does more educating than the schools and all the institutions of higher learning.*

—Marshall McLuhan
(Canadian author, educator, and philosopher, 1911–1980)

◆ *Television is an invention that permits you to be entertained in your living room by people you wouldn't have in your home.*

—David Frost (English TV talk show host, b. 1939)

Work in your groups to discuss your feelings about television. Is television educational? Is it the first truly democratic culture? Is it child's play or chewing gum for the eyes? Provide examples to support your opinions.

BEYOND THE CLASSROOM

Use the Internet to research the kinds of reality TV programs currently on the air. Then work with three to four other students to develop a reality TV program of your own. Describe the type of contestants or participants you want on the show, what you want them to do, and what the theme or goal of the show will be. When all the groups are done, take turns presenting your ideas to the class. Discuss the pros and cons of each idea. Talk about which shows you would consider watching and why.

Judging by Appearances

THINKING ABOUT THE TOPIC

Talk in small groups or with the whole class.

1. Which workplace appears to be casual, creative, and unconventional? Describe some of the details on which you based your opinion.

2. Which workplace appears to be traditional, conservative, or corporate? Describe some details on which you based your opinion.

3. Which type of environment would you feel most comfortable working in? Why?

TALKING ABOUT YOUR EXPERIENCE

How much does personal appearance affect the way we perceive ourselves and others? Do our clothes, jewelry, and hairdos truly express who we are? Should we worry about other people's perceptions of our personal appearance?

Assess your attitudes about the importance of personal appearance. Read and respond to each statement. Write 1 if you agree, 2 if you are neutral, and 3 if you disagree.

1. __1__ Clothes say a lot about a person.

2. __2__ People should be able to dress however they like.

3. __1__ It is important to dress appropriately for certain situations.

4. __3__ It is fair to judge people by to their clothes.

Discuss with a partner.

1. How were you and your partner's attitudes about personal appearance similar? different? Discuss one item about which you disagreed.

2. Why do you feel the way you do about personal appearance? Does your cultural background or family influence your attitudes about clothing? Explain.

LISTENING

Preparing to Listen

You are about to listen to a conversation between a student and a career counselor. Answer the questions before you listen. Discuss your answers as a class.

1. Do you think that it is necessary to dress a certain way to perform specific jobs well?

2. Is there a standard dress code for job interviews in your home country?

Listening for Details

Look over the statements. Listen to the conversation at least twice. As you listen, mark the statements as true (T) or false (F). If a statement is false, correct it to make it true.

1. __T__ The student is taking Mr. Mason's class this semester.

2. __F__ The student has been applying for jobs and sending out résumés.

3. __T__ The student needs help with his interviewing technique.

4. __T__ Only one company called the student back after he went for an interview.

5. __F__ The counselor thinks the student may be overqualified for these jobs.

6. __T__ The student wore a suit and tie to the job interviews.

7. __T__ The counselor says the student may have to choose between his appearance and a job.

8. __T__ The student thinks he'd be happier working for a company that had a dress code.

Responding to the Listening

Discuss the questions in small groups.

1. Did the counselor give the student good advice? Explain.

2. Would you be willing to change your appearance or style of dressing to get a job? How much would you be willing to change?

3. Do you think it is fair for employers to dictate how employees dress at work? Why?

WORDS AND PHRASES ABOUT PERSONAL APPEARANCE

Work with a partner to complete the sentences using the words and phrases from the box. Use a dictionary if necessary.

you do what everybody does

attire	chic	cosmetics	demeanor	physical	trendy

1. No matter what fashion fads are popular, my sister has a great sense of what looks attractive and stylish on her. Everyone agrees that she is very ___Chic___ chic

2. We often judge people by the way they behave, dress, and speak. We make judgments about their character based on their ___demeanor___ .

3. The ___cosmetics___ industry makes a lot of money selling creams, powders, and other products that are supposed to make people's skin and body look more attractive.

4. Certain people are influenced by the latest styles in fashion. For these people, it is very important to wear the latest clothes and to look ___trendy___ .

5. Fashion magazines and advertisements place a great deal of emphasis on ___physical___ beauty. iner

6. At this bank, the appropriate ___attire___ for male employees is a suit and tie.

Work with a partner. Match the informal expressions on the left with their definitions on the right. Write the letter on the line. Use a dictionary if necessary.

1. __e__ dress down   casual

2. __a__ dress up

3. __d__ evening wear

4. __c__ fashion plate

5. __b__ fashion statement

    a. to wear clothes that are more formal than you would usually wear

    b. an unusual way of wearing clothes that makes people notice you and shows them what your feelings, attitudes, or opinions are

    c. someone who likes to wear very fashionable clothes

    d. special clothes you wear for formal occasions at night

    e. to wear clothes that are less formal than the ones you usually wear

PROBLEM SOLVING

Read and listen to each problem. Then look at the possible solutions given and add some of your own. Decide what you would do in each case. Write the reasons for your decision.

Problem 1

Your school has a policy of "no visible tattoos." You come from a culture in which tattoos are very common and considered beautiful. You have many visible tattoos that you could cover by dressing in long sleeves and long pants at all times. What do you do?

1. Explain that tattoos are considered beautiful in your culture and hope that the school administration will see your point of view.

2. Wear clothes that cover your tattoos to respect the school's policy.

3. _____

4. _____

Reasons: _____

_____

Problem 2

You are on a jury. One member of the jury has taken an instant dislike to the defendant because he objects to the defendant's appearance. He says that the defendant must be guilty because he "looks sneaky and wears an earring." You think that the juror is making an unfair judgment, which has nothing to do with the evidence in the case. What do you do?

1. Try to convince the juror to overcome his initial prejudices.

2. Go to the defense attorney and explain the situation.

3. _____

4. _____

Reasons: _____

_____

physical

You have to attend a formal family affair. You know that many of the men and women there will be dressed up in traditional evening clothes, but you don't like to dress that way. Your parents don't object to your casual "dressed down" style, but some of the older members of the family, such as your grandparents, certainly will. What do you do?

1. Dress up this time like everyone else.

2. Go as you please.

3. _____

4. _____

Reasons: _____

_____

Work in small groups. Talk about each of the previous problems and decide what your group would do. Try to use some of the words and phrases about personal appearance on page 60.

FROM THE NEWS

Preparing to Read

Answer the questions before you read. Discuss the answers as a class.

1. Have you ever had to wear a school uniform or do you know of schools that require uniforms? What do you think about such policies?

2. If you wore a uniform, did you like it? Why?

School Uniforms: Quick Fix or Bad Call?

Ann Svensen

There is something comforting about schoolchildren dressed in pleats and plaid. Maybe it reminds us of our own childhood, or **conjures up** thoughts of order and safety. Whatever the reason, one thing's for sure—school uniforms are getting a lot of wear these days.

From California to Boston, some of the nation's largest school districts now have uniform policies. In New York City alone, more than half a million elementary-school students will be wearing them by next fall.

A CASE FOR UNIFORMS

No long-term, formal studies have been done on the effectiveness of school uniforms, but many schools have kept their own informal statistics. California's Long Beach Unified School District's records are probably cited most often. This urban district **adopted** a **mandatory** uniform policy in 1994. Since then, school crime has dropped by 76 percent, while attendance has reached an all-time high.

IF YOU'RE A SKEPTIC, GET IN LINE

But Long Beach's glowing statistics have been met with **skepticism.** Some education experts say that no school can prove that uniforms alone cause such dramatic reductions in crime. Other detractors [1] see uniform policies as a violation of students' rights to free expression, and nothing more than a Band-Aid that fails to address the real causes of youth violence.

PROS AND CONS

Dr. Alan Hilfer, senior psychologist in the Children's and Adolescent Unit at Maimonides Medical Center in Brooklyn says, "Uniforms do eliminate competition, pressure, and assaults[2] **perpetrated** by older kids on younger kids for their sneakers and other possessions. They also allow some kids to focus better, especially in the lower grades." But Dr. Hilfer says there is a **downside:** "Clothes are a source of expression for children, and as kids get older, they become increasingly **resentful** of uniforms."

FROM THE TRENCHES

Anthony Poet, assistant principal at the Pueblo Del Sol Middle School in Arizona, recently **instituted** a uniform policy in his school. He's the first to agree that kids don't like uniforms. But he noticed that the same kids who said they hated the policy also said they're glad to have it. One student confirms, "Uniforms make the school safer, but I don't like them."

Since his school began requiring uniforms, Poet has documented a remarkable drop in discipline problems. But until a long-term study is done, he says he can't be sure whether it's the uniforms or the act of instituting the policy that's made the difference. Dr. Hilfer explains: "Discipline problems may be decreasing in schools with uniforms because the schools (and the parents) have begun taking the issue of discipline more seriously."

ARE UNIFORMS RIGHT FOR YOUR DISTRICT?

According to Dr. Hilfer, strict dress codes are not for everybody. "Some schools **thrive on** permissiveness and individuality, while others have to be more **restrictive** to contain a restless student body." Before making the uniform decision, he suggests that schools carefully consider their unique populations; what kind of message they want to send; and whether or not they think their kids will go for it. Dr. Hilfer warns, "By instituting a uniform policy, schools are taking away kids' individuality—schools need to decide if that sacrifice is worth making."

---

[1] *detractors:* people who say bad things about someone or something in order to make it seem less good than they really are

[2] *assaults:* violent, physical attacks on someone

Checking Your Comprehension

Mark the statement as true (T) or false (F) according to the information and opinions in the article. If a statement is false, correct it to make it true.

1. ____ There have been formal studies on the effectiveness of school uniforms.

2. ____ One school district documented a drop in crime after requiring students to wear uniforms.

3. _____ Some people think school uniforms violate students' right to free expression.

4. _____ Some students think uniforms do make a school safer.

5. _____ Strict dress codes are a good idea for all types of schools and student populations.

Thinking Critically About the Reading

Discuss in small groups. Then share your responses with the class.

1. Based on the article you just read, would you want your children to wear school uniforms? Why?

2. Why might uniforms have a positive effect on school atmosphere? What is it about wearing uniforms that creates a safer and less competitive school environment?

3. Do you think that uniforms limit students' expression and individuality? Why?

4. When you see someone in a uniform, for example a nurse or bus driver, does it change how you react? Why?

WORDS AND PHRASES FROM THE READING

Look at the words in the box. Find them in boldface print in the news article on page 63. Look at the context of each word. Can you figure out the meaning?

adopted	conjures up	downside	instituted	mandatory
perpetrated	resentful	restrictive	skepticism	thrive on

Read the sentences, which are based on the news article about uniforms. Circle the letter of the best meaning for each underlined word. Use a dictionary if necessary.

1. One school district <u>adopted</u> a uniform policy in 1994.
   a. made a child legally part of a family that he or she was not born into
   b. chosen to use or consider as your own, e.g., a country, name, or religion
   c. started to use a particular method or plan for dealing with something

2. Uniforms might remind us of our own childhood, or <u>conjure up</u> thoughts of order and safety.
   a. to bring a thought, picture, idea, or memory to someone's mind
   b. to make something appear when it is not expected
   c. to make the spirit of a dead person appear

3. One <u>downside</u> to school uniforms is that some children like to use clothes to express themselves.
   a. the negative part or disadvantage of something
   b. the lower side of something
   c. the reason for something

4. More and more schools have <u>instituted</u> uniform policies in their schools.
   a. organized for a particular purpose
   b. introduced or started
   c. enlarged or extended

5. One way to get all students to dress alike is to have a <u>mandatory</u> uniform policy.
   a. freely chosen
   b. suggested
   c. required by authority; compulsory

6. Sometimes assaults in school are <u>perpetrated</u> by older kids on younger kids.
   a. made a situation, attitude, etc., continue to exist
   b. carried out or committed something seriously wrong or criminal
   c. done something as an older child

7. Parents and teachers do not want children to be <u>resentful</u> of uniform policies; that would create more problems.
   a. angry or upset about something that you think is unfair
   b. too attached to something
   c. disobedient of a new rule

8. Some see school uniforms as <u>restrictive</u> because students cannot choose what to wear to school.
   a. confusing
   b. allowing choice
   c. controlling, limiting

9. There is some <u>skepticism</u> about whether school uniforms really do control behavior; some people have a lot of doubts.
   a. a desire to control others' behavior
   b. a strong belief in uniform policies
   c. an attitude of doubt about whether something is true, right, or good

10. Many people <u>thrive on</u> expressing themselves freely and that helps make students happier and more successful in school; wearing uniforms would take that away.
    a. to become more outspoken about your beliefs
    b. to discuss something thoroughly
    c. to enjoy or be successful

Match the phrases on the left with their meanings on the right. Use a dictionary if necessary.

1. _____ free expression   a. accept something

2. _____ go for it   b. the right to say and do what you think

3. _____ the trenches   c. the place or situation where most of the work or action in an activity takes place

CONVERSATION TIP

How do you express your disappointment, react to someone else's disappointment, or present an alternate point of view? Here are some words and phrases you can use to express disappointment and respond to the disappointments of others.

SPEAKING ABOUT DISAPPOINTMENT	
Expressing Disappointment	*Reacting to Disappointment*
I was really looking forward to . . .	Sorry to hear that.
I really had my mind set on . . .	That's too bad/a shame.
It's too bad that . . .	Sometimes these things happen.
I'm disappointed that . . .	It's out of your control.
I'm troubled because . . .	Try not to take it personally.
I feel crushed.	Things have a way of working out.

OFFERING ANOTHER VIEW
You could always . . .
Look at it this way . . .
It could be worse. What if you had to . . .
In the overall scheme of things, it's not as bad as you think.

ACT IT OUT

Work with a partner. Use the conversation tip expressions in the box and the words and phrases from the unit to act out the following role play.

Situation

You just found out that your new job has a dress code. The appropriate attire that is required is very different from the way you like to dress. You now have a lot of clothes you won't be able to wear and must go shopping for new clothes. Describe the new work situation, how you must dress, how you feel about not being able to dress as you like, and why. Your partner must respond to your disappointment and offer another view of the situation.

> **EXAMPLE**
>
> **Student A:** *I just got this great new job.*
>
> **Student B:** *That's great!*
>
> **Student A:** *Yes, but there's one drawback. You know those trendy new clothes I just bought? I was really looking forward to wearing them, but now I can't.*
>
> **Student B:** *That's too bad. But why?*
>
> **Student A:** *The company has a strict dress code.*

PROVERBS AND SAYINGS ABOUT APPEARANCE

There are many famous sayings about appearance. Read and discuss the meaning of each proverb and quotation in small groups. Compare the sayings. In what ways are they similar? In what ways do they agree or disagree with your own beliefs about personal appearance and inner worth?

◆ *First appearance deceives many.*

—Ovid
(Poet, 43 B.C.–A.D. 17)

◆ *Things do not pass for what they are, but for what they seem. Most things are judged by their jackets.*

—Baltasar Gracián
(Spanish Jesuit philosopher and writer, 1601–1658)

◆ *Outside show is a poor substitute for inner worth.*

—Aesop
(Ancient Greek composer of fables, ca. 620 B.C.–560 B.C.)

◆ *Do not judge by appearances; a rich heart may be under a poor coat.*

—Gaelic Proverb

BEYOND THE CLASSROOM

Use the Internet to research tattoos. Write a short essay about your findings. Use these questions to help guide your research:

- Where and when did tattoos originate?
- Where have tattoos been used throughout the world?
- What was the original purpose of tattoos? What other purposes have they served?
- How have tattoos evolved historically?
- What is the significance of tattoos in various cultures?
- How did tattoos become part of popular culture today?

What Is the Value of Money?

THINKING ABOUT THE TOPIC

Talk in small groups or with the whole class.

1. What does each photograph show about the value of money?

2. If you were given $20,000 and had to spend it on one of these two things, which would you choose? Why?

3. What does this say about your values when it comes to money?

TALKING ABOUT YOUR EXPERIENCE

Everyone has a different view about how money should be spent and what the true value of money is. Some people think it is best to live modestly and save for the future. Others would rather live well now, and not worry about tomorrow. Some people think you get what you pay for. They would rather spend money to buy the best of everything. Others worry about cost. They try to buy items on sale or select items with a lower price.

What are your values when it comes to money? Think about each of these situations. Circle your choice and write your reason.

1. You have received a $100 bonus at work. You are in your twenties, living on a budget, with limited savings. What do you do?
   a. Spend it now on something you want but don't really need.
   b. Invest it in the hope that it will grow to $1,000 in ten years.
   Reason: _____

2. You are in your fifties and hope to retire early. You have very little savings but receive a good salary for the work you do. You need a car to get to work. What do you do?
   a. Take out a new car loan, buy a new car, and make high monthly payments to pay the car off over five years.
   b. Buy a used car that is cheaper than the price of the new one and pay it off in a year.
   Reason: _____

3. You are in your thirties. You have a credit card and need some new clothes for your job. You are living on a tight budget. What do you do?
   a. Buy whatever you want right away and make the minimum payment on your credit card bill every month.
   b. Improve your wardrobe slowly. Only buy the clothes you can actually pay for each month.
   Reason: _____

4. You are in your twenties and working in the heart of the city. You need an apartment but rents in the city are high. What do you do?
   a. Pay the cost of the high rent because you want to live close to work and be in the center of the action.
   b. Find an apartment in a nearby suburb that is a lot cheaper and commute an hour each way to work.
   Reason: _____

Discuss with a partner.

1. How were you and your partner's money decisions similar? How were they different? Discuss one situation in which you responded differently. Try to explain your reasoning to your partner.

2. Compare your general attitudes about how money should be spent. What did you learn about the value you place on money? Was time more important to you than money? Was money in the present more important to you than money in the future?

3. What effect, if any, did age have on your choices? Explain.

LISTENING

Preparing to Listen

You are about to listen to a conversation between two old friends about the value of money. Answer the questions before you listen. Discuss your answers as a class.

1. If you became a millionaire tomorrow, what would you do? Would you alter your lifestyle? If so, how?

2. If you had to donate a million dollars to a single project or cause, what would it be? Why?

3. Do you think that people with millions or even billions of dollars should share some of their wealth with people who are less fortunate? Why?

Listening for Details

Look over the statements. Listen to the conversation at least twice. As you listen, circle the letter of the best answer to complete the sentences.

1. Gretchen and Mick haven't seen each other in _b_.
   a. two weeks   **b.** a long time

2. Mick used to _b_ for Virginia Stone.
   a. do painting   **b.** shovel snow

3. No one in the neighborhood realized that Virginia was _b_.
   a. an artist   **b.** a multi-millionaire

4. Virginia has been donating a lot of money to help _b_.
   a. established artists   **b.** struggling artists at the beginning of their careers

5. Mick thinks that Virginia's behavior is _a_ a millionaire.
   a. unusual for   **b.** typical of

6. Gretchen thinks that millionaires who hold on to their money are _b_.
   a. show offs   **b.** greedy

7. Mick thinks that Gretchen's point of view about millionaires is _a_.
   a. too simplistic   **b.** realistic

8. If Mick became a millionaire, he would _b_.
   a. donate money to help refugees   **b.** buy things for himself

9. The rock star Bono committed time and money to help improve health care and education in _b_.
   a. Cambodia   **b.** Africa

10. Angelina Jolie worked as the Goodwill Ambassador for __b__ on behalf of refugees.
   a. the United States   **b.** the United Nations

11. Gretchen thinks rich people __a__ have an obligation to share their money with people who are less fortunate.
   a. do   **b.** don't

Responding to the Listening

Actress Angelina Jolie distributes soccer balls at a refugee camp on the Thai-Burma border.

Discuss the questions in small groups.

1. Do you approve of what Virginia Stone is doing with her money? Why?

2. Do you think that supporting arts organizations is as important as helping people who need basic food, shelter, and clothing? Why?

3. How would you define *greed*? Do you agree with Mick or with Gretchen about the superrich? Explain.

4. Do you think that millionaires and billionaires have a moral responsibility to share some of their wealth with others? Why?

5. Do you admire what Bono and Angelina Jolie have done with their money and fame? Why?

WORDS AND PHRASES ABOUT MONEY

Work with a partner. Read the sentences. For each item, choose the word from the box that has the same meaning as the underlined words. Use a dictionary if necessary. The first one has been done for you.

hoard	means	nest egg	set aside	~~spendthrift~~	stingy

1. ___spendthrift___ I am a <u>person who spends money carelessly</u>. I would like to change that bad habit.

2. ___nest egg___ My parents had a <u>certain amount of money saved</u> before they retired.

3. ___stingy___ Some people are <u>not generous with money</u> even when they have a lot of it.

4. ___the means to___ I have the <u>money or income that I need</u> to pay all my bills and save some too.

5. ___set aside___ I plan to buy a house, so I have <u>kept money and other resources especially for that purpose</u>; when the time is right, I'll have the amount I need.

6. ___hoard___ My brother used to <u>collect and hide large amounts of</u> money in an old trunk in the basement.

Work with a partner. Match the informal idioms and expressions on the left with their definitions on the right. Write the letter on the line. Use a dictionary if necessary.

1. __c__ a dime a dozen
2. __d__ living the high life
3. __a__ be on a shoestring
4. __b__ spare no expense

   a. to do something without spending much money

   b. to spend as much money as necessary to make something really good, even if it is a lot

   c. very common and not valuable

   d. enjoying yourself by going out often and spending a lot of money

Work with a partner. Use the words and phrases about money to complete the conversation. When you are done, practice reading aloud the dialogue with your partner.

1. **A:** I notice you like to go out a lot; it seems as if you go out to a different restaurant every night. How can you afford that?

   B: I just think you should enjoy life so that's what I am doing. I'm ___high life___. Why don't you come with me sometime? I'll pay. I spend money on my friends all the time. I'm not at all ___stingy___ .

2. **A:** I guess we just have different values when it comes to money. You like to live in the moment, and I worry about the future. Instead of spending the limited amount of money I have on fancy dinners, I prefer to save it. Eventually, I want to buy a house.

B: Well, you can _set aside_ money to buy a house but I'd rather live in a cheap apartment and be able to go out to shows and fancy restaurants and buy nice clothes. I want to enjoy life now. I don't spend much time worrying about the future.

3. **A:** You must have a good job if you have the _means_ to pay all your bills and still live the way you do.

   B: When it comes to enjoyment, I will spend whatever it takes; I don't worry about what it costs. I _spare no expense_ when it comes to enjoying myself. If I want something, I buy it. I don't think about retirement and all that.

4. **A:** So you haven't saved up some money for retirement. You don't have a _nest egg_?

   B: No. I don't believe in saving. Why should I _hoard_ my money? What's the value in that?

5. **A:** Well, I do hope you're at least careful with the money you have.

   B: Don't misunderstand me. I'm a careful shopper with a lot of consumer know-how. I'm not a _spendthrift_. I know exactly what I am buying and I choose carefully. Take my shirt, for instance. It's expensive but very well made.

6. **A:** Well, I'm a student so I am _living on a shoestring When I go on vacation_. I buy most of my clothes at thrift shops, for now, anyway. After I graduate, I'll get a good job and all that will change.

   B: Don't you have a big student loan? You'll be paying that back for a while.

7. **A:** Yes, but in the long run, it's worth it. I will have a good career. To me, clothes, cars, and eating out are unimportant. I want to invest in my mind and my future. Material items are _a dime a dozen_, and I don't need them.

   B: Well, we are all so different. That's what makes life interesting! So let's go get something to eat.

PROBLEM SOLVING

Read and listen to each problem. Then look at the possible solutions given and add some of your own. Decide what you would do in each case. Write the reasons for your decision.

P r o b l e m 1

You often go out to dinner with a group of friends. When the bill arrives, everyone is supposed to pay his or her fair share. Recently, though, when you added up the money, there wasn't enough. You determined that one friend in particular is not paying the right amount. She is unemployed right now and may not have the money to pay her share. What do you do?

1. Pay the extra amount yourself without saying anything to anyone.

2. Confront the friend publicly about not paying her share of the bill.

3. _____

4. _____

Reasons: _____

_____

Problem 2

You are spending the day visiting with a friend who is telling you about her money problems. She has gotten herself into debt, and is worried about paying it off. While you are walking with her, you pass an expensive clothing store. She sees something inside she wants, but says, "Oh, I can't afford that." Then she goes inside to buy it. What do you do?

1. Not say anything.

2. Encourage her to think twice before she buys anything.

3. _____

4. _____

Reasons: _____

_____

Problem 3

You have been looking for a job and have finally received two job offers. Both jobs are in your field. One offers a very high salary but will require you to work at night and on weekends. The other pays less but would give you your nights and weekends free. What do you do?

1. Try to negotiate a better situation for the job that pays more.

2. Take the job that pays less.

3. _____

4. _____

Reasons: _____

_____

Work in small groups. Talk about each of the previous problems and decide what your group would do. Try to use some of the words and phrases about money on page 72.

FROM THE NEWS

Preparing to Read

Answer the questions before you read. Discuss your answers as a class.

1. What millionaires or billionaires have you read or heard about in the news recently? Name a few of them.

2. What are some ways that people become multimillionaires?

3. What percentage of wealthy people worldwide do you think inherit their money?

Billionaires Are a Dime a Dozen

By Peter Josty, Calgary Herald

Forbes magazine[1] has published its list of the world's richest people in 2001. It lists 538 billionaires in 46 countries. If you look around the world, some countries have many individuals on this list, some none at all. Why is this? Do you get to be very rich because of your genes, or because of where you live? And what aspect of where you live influences this? Let's see what the billionaires list can tell us about that, and about how Canada fares.

People get on this list for one of two reasons— they inherit money from someone, or they make it themselves. Sometimes they do both, but not often.

INHERITANCE

We calculated what **proportion** of billionaires inherited their wealth. This gives us a rough and ready sense of the possibilities for upward mobility in a country. In the United States, roughly 40 percent inherited their wealth. In Europe, which generally has a somewhat more rigid social structure, and much less history of being **entrepreneurial**, many more inherited their money. In France, two thirds of the billionaires inherited their money, and in the United Kingdom exactly the same proportion. The Duke of Westminster—who is a **remnant** of the feudal **aristocracy**—is still the richest man in Britain, mainly because of his ownership of land, including the 300 acres on which the City of London was built. Canada, as so often seems to happen, falls halfway between the United States and Europe, with about 50 percent inheriting their money.

INNOVATION

Of the self-made billionaires, some (such as Warren Buffett—a U.S. investor) got on the list because they are **astute** investors. But the vast majority get there because they **pioneered** something new and useful, in other words, because they were innovators. Of the ten richest people, eight **indisputably** got there because of an **innovation**, a new product or service that met people's needs better then what went before. Three of these were "high tech"—Bill Gates and Paul Allen from Microsoft, and Larry Ellison from Oracle, but interestingly five were from retailing—four members of the Walton family whose wealth came from Wal-Mart, and two

brothers who founded the Aldi discount store. The remaining two were Warren Buffett, whose wealth came from investing, and a Saudi Prince who inherited money. The innovators represent all **sectors** of the economy—and are certainly not just in the "high tech" area. Creative risk takers seem to be rewarded.

CLIMATE FOR INNOVATION

We can try and compare countries by devising a statistic we'll call: "self-made billionaires per million population." This gives a rough and ready sense of the climate for innovation in each country. As before, Canada (0.3) falls between the United States (0.5) and Europe (0.07–0.08). Astonishingly, this ranking agrees exactly with the results of a major international study called the Global Entrepreneurship Monitor, coordinated from Babson College, in the United States. This study carried out extensive surveys to find out what proportion of the population was involved in entrepreneurial activities.

BILLIONAIRES IN CANADA

There are 16 billionaires in Canada. About half of them inherited their wealth, with names like Thomson, Irving, Weston, Bronfman, and McCain. Several immigrants are on the list, including Terry Matthews who founded Newbridge Networks and Michael Lee-Chin who founded AIC, a mutual fund company. There are also several **emigrants**, including Jeff Skoll, founder of eBay,[2] who now lives in Silicon Valley. As in so many other ways, Canada finds itself between the United States and Europe in its number of billionaires.

NATURE OR NURTURE?

The distribution of billionaires around the world seems to reflect the underlying economic, social, and cultural characteristics of different countries, rather than a random scattering of exceptional genes. Countries that have a relatively open social structure and that accept and reward enterprising behavior seem to produce more rich people. So where you happen to be born plays a big part in determining success. Some billionaires recognize this in their more humble moments. Bill Gates was quoted recently as saying that he had been lucky, not in the sense of finding something, but in the sense of being born in a time and place that allowed him to exercise his talents to the full.

---

[1] *Forbes magazine:* a financial and business news magazine
[2] *eBay:* an online "marketplace" where people can buy, sell, and trade items

Checking Your Comprehension

Scan the news article for the answers to these questions, and write your responses.

1. How many billionaires in how many countries were listed in 2001?

   _____ 46 Contr _____

2. What are the two main ways that people become billionaires?

   _____ gean X where you live _____

3. In each of the following countries, what percentage of people inherited their money?

   United States _240%_

   France _²/₃_ 66%

   United Kingdom _66%_

   Canada _50%_

4. How did people who did *not* inherit their money become billionaires?

   _____ made it themselves _____

5. How does where you are born contribute to your likelihood of becoming a billionaire?

   _____

   _____

Thinking Critically About the Reading

Discuss in small groups. Then share your responses with the class.

1. Whom do you admire more—a person who becomes rich because of an innovation or someone who becomes rich because of shrewd investments? Why?

2. Do you think there should be laws restricting the amount a person can inherit? Why?

3. Why might countries with open social structures produce more rich people?

WORDS AND PHRASES FROM THE READING

Look at the words below. Find them in boldface print in the news article on page 75. Look at the context of each word. Can you figure out the meaning? Match the words on the left with their meanings on the right. Use a dictionary if necessary.

1. __F__ aristocracy

2. __c__ astute

3. __e__ emigrants

4. __a__ entrepreneurial

5. __b__ indisputably

6. __i__ innovation

7. __h__ pioneered

a. capable of starting a company, arranging business deals, and taking risks in order to make a profit

b. definitely; without question

c. able to understand situations or behavior very well and very quickly, especially so that you can be successful

d. parts of an area of activity, especially of business or trade

e. a part or share of a larger amount or number of something

8. __e__ proportion

9. __j__ remnant

10. __d__ sectors

f. the people in the highest social class who, traditionally, have a lot of land, money, and power

g. people who leave their own country to live in another country

h. did, invented, or used something before anyone else

i. a new idea, method, or invention

j. a small part of something that remains after the rest of it is gone

Read the sentences. Circle the letter of the best meaning for the underlined phrase.

1. <u>Risk takers</u> are often rewarded for their ability to try new, potentially risky things, by receiving financial benefits.
   a. people who will do something that involves some danger in order to achieve something
   b. people who earn money by doing dangerous things

2. I wanted to plan a spectacular party for a friend but I ran out of time. I had to do a lot of things quickly and not as well as I would have liked. It was a <u>rough and ready</u> way to plan a party, but everyone had a good time.
   a. perfect for a particular situation
   b. not perfect for a particular situation, but good enough

3. I admire <u>self-made</u> millionaires, people who have achieved success and wealth through their own intelligence and creativity.
   a. having achieved success and wealth through inheritance
   b. having achieved success and wealth through one's own efforts

4. Inheriting money is certainly one way to achieve <u>upward mobility</u> into a higher social class.
   a. the ability to move up through social classes and become richer
   b. the ability to invest money successfully

CONVERSATION TIP

Sometimes a person says or does something that completely surprises you—so much so that you can't believe it is happening. Here are some ways to show surprise and disbelief and to react to it in someone else.

Showing Surprise and Disbelief	*Responding to Surprise and Disbelief*
You're kidding!/You've got to be kidding!	I know it's difficult to believe, but it's true.
Why would you . . . ?	I'm not making this up.
That's staggering news.	I've thought it through and this is my
That's beyond belief.	decision.
I'm astounded/amazed/taken aback.	The reality is . . .
	It's a fact.
	Take my word for it.

ACT IT OUT

Act out the situation with a partner. Use the conversation tip expressions in the box and the words and phrases from the unit to act out the following role play.

Situation

Student A: You must tell your friend that you have recently inherited a large amount of money. After your describe the details, explain that you have decided to donate all of the money to a charitable organization of some kind. Tell your friend why you have chosen to donate the money instead of keeping it for yourself. Your friend is going to act surprised, and you will have to respond to his/her disbelief.

Student B: Express your surprise about your friend's inheritance and your disbelief about the decision to donate all the money to charity. Question your friend's reasoning. For example, you might say: *Why would you want to give all that money away? Don't you want to share some of it with family members or use it to travel?*

PROVERBS ABOUT MONEY

Explore proverbs about money. Read and discuss the meaning of each proverb in small groups.

> ◆ *Too much prosperity makes most men fools.*
>
> —Italian Proverb
>
> ◆ *Money spent on the mind is never spent in vain.*
>
> —Traditional Proverb
>
> ◆ *Before borrowing money from a friend, decide which you need most.*
>
> —American Proverb
>
> ◆ *With money you can build a road in the sea.*
>
> —Maltese Proverb

Select one proverb and describe to your classmates a situation in which it applies. Try to locate other proverbs about money from other parts of the world. Share them with the class.

BEYOND THE CLASSROOM

Continue to explore the unit theme by completing the following activities.

1. Use the Internet to look up a billionaire. Some billionaires you might want to consider are Warren Buffett, Bill Gates, Prince Alwaleed Bin Talal Alsaud, and Alice Walton. Try searching by the keyword "billionaires" or "billionaires + (your country name)" or use the names of one of the people above. Find out how the billionaire made his or her money and what the person's philosophy is regarding wealth and spending. Then have a class discussion in which you compare and contrast your subjects. Discuss which billionaires you admire and which ones you do not, and explain why.

2. Imagine you had ten minutes to talk to a billionaire. What would you ask him or her? Make a list of ten questions. Then compare your questions with your classmates'.

(handwritten notes)
- our is save money
- for other makeing biger other company.
- how the billionaire made his
- person's philosophy.
- Where he live
- hobbies
- family

How Important Are Family Ties?

THINKING ABOUT THE TOPIC

Talk in small groups or with the whole class.

1. Describe what the woman is doing or feeling in each picture.
2. What kind of decisions do you think the woman is trying to make?
3. Why do you think the woman is pulled in so many directions?

TALKING ABOUT YOUR EXPERIENCE

In many parts of the world people live at home until they marry. This is often for economic or social reasons. In the United States and in Western Europe, it's common for young adults to leave home when they go to college and live on their own after that.

Work in small groups. Brainstorm advantages and disadvantages of living with your family after you reach adulthood. Write your ideas on the chart. Then number the items in each column in terms of their importance. Use "1" for the most important advantage and disadvantage.

Advantages of Living at Home with Family	Disadvantages of Living at Home with Family
- no small rent - suport each other - don't feel alone - share hosehold respon— - siblites - safe	- not as much privecy - follow rules - less responsible - argumants 647 7659272 09114 51212 tady 01125 19 111 7 1 4 7 1

Discuss with the class.

1. According to your group, what was the number one advantage to living with your family? What was the number one disadvantage? Are you surprised by the other groups' answers? Explain.

2. Did the male and female students have a different view about living at home? Explain.

3. Why do some people decide to leave home? Why do some decide to stay?

LISTENING

Preparing to Listen

You are about to listen to a conversation about living close to home and family or moving away. Answer the questions before you listen. Discuss your answers with the class.

1. What is the living situation of your closest friends? Do most of them live with or near their parents? In general, do you think they enjoy being close to their families or not? Explain.

2. Why do some parents want their adult children to live close to them?

Listening for Details

Look over the questions. Then listen to the conversation at least twice. As you listen, write down your answers to the questions. You do not need to write complete sentences. Just take notes.

1. What are the man's plans after college?

   _____

2. What are the woman's plans after college?

   _____

3. How does the woman describe her relationship to her family?

   _____

4. How does the man feel about his family?

   _____

5. What does the woman think about the man's career choice? Why?

   _____

6. What does the man think about young people moving away? Why?

   _____

Responding to the Listening

Discuss the questions in small groups.

1. Do you think that an adult has a responsibility to stay close to family even if it means not taking advantage of all the opportunities available to him or her? Explain.

2. If you come from a family with more than one child, is one child expected to stay closer to home than another? Explain.

3. Do you foresee staying close to your family or moving away? Why?

4. At what age is it easiest to move away from home? Why?

WORDS AND PHRASES ABOUT FAMILIES

Work with a partner to complete the sentences using the words from the box. Use a dictionary if necessary.

ancestor	blood relation	descendants	domestic	matriarchal	patriarchal

1. Some people enjoy various aspects of ___domestic___ life, such as cooking, cleaning, and spending time at home.

2. Men control things and have all the power in ___patriarchal___ societies.

3. Someone related to you by birth rather than by marriage is a ___blood relation___

4. We did research on a relative who lived in the 1700s and found out a lot of information about this ___ancestor___ of ours.

5. In a _Patriarchal_ family or social system, women are the rulers or the ones in control.

6. Your children and your children's children are your _descendants_

Work with a partner. Match the words and phrases on the left with their definitions on the right. Write the letter on the line. Use a dictionary if necessary.

1. _b_ extended family
2. _d_ in-laws
3. _a_ nuclear family
4. _c_ single-parent family

a. a family unit that consists only of husband, wife, and children

b. a family group that includes not only parents and children but also grandparents, aunts, uncles, etc.

c. a family in which only a mother or a father takes care of the children, without a partner

d. your relatives by marriage, especially the father and mother of your husband or wife

Work with a partner. Tell your partner about your family background and the type of family you grew up in. You can give an actual description or make one up. Your description should answer the following questions:

1. What do you know about your ancestors? Where did they come from originally? What languages did they speak? What did they do for a living?

2. In your culture, are families matriarchal or patriarchal? Explain.

3. Did you grow up in a nuclear or an extended family? How many people lived in your household? What are the advantages and disadvantages of nuclear families? Extended families?

4. What are your in-laws like? Describe one of them.

5. What three things would you like to pass on to your descendants? Why?

PROBLEM SOLVING

Read and listen to each problem. Then look at the possible solutions given and add some of your own. Decide what you would do in each case. Write the reasons for your decision.

Problem 1

You are a woman who has just had a child. You grew up in an extended family. When your older sister had her baby, your grandmother came and lived with her so that your sister could go back to work. Your grandmother wants to give you the same kind of assistance, and you are eager for her to come and live with you for several months. However, your husband doesn't like the idea. He grew up in a nuclear family and is an only child. He places a great deal of value on privacy. He says that you should simply hire a babysitter when you return to work. You don't want to leave your baby alone with a stranger. What do you do?

1. Try to convince your husband to let your grandmother come and live with you for a while.

2. Try to find a babysitter you like and can trust.

3. _____

4. _____

Reasons: _____

_____

Problem 2

Your family eats dinner together every night. It is the only time that you are all together. Over dinner, your parents encourage you and your siblings to share information about your lives, school, work, and anything else that's going on. They believe that coming together for dinner is a good way for family members to remain close. You are seventeen and want to be able to go out with your friends for dinner and enjoy other activities when you feel like it. You find the company of your friends much more stimulating than being with your family. What do you do?

1. Have dinner with your family during the week, but go out with your friends on the weekend.

2. Tell your family that you have outgrown the tradition of having dinner together.

3. _____

4. _____

Reasons: _____

_____

Your grandparents have been running a music store for fifty years. They started the business from scratch and are very proud of it. The store is very successful and brings in a lot of income. They have reached retirement age and want you, and only you, to take over the business. You have just completed your degree in music, are an excellent cellist, and are eager to start your new career as a professional musician. You would like to be in an orchestra that tours internationally. You are very fond of your grandparents, but you are not interested in working in the music shop. What do you do?

1. Encourage your grandparents to sell the music store.

2. Agree to take over your grandparents' music store and play the cello in your free time.

3. _____

4. _____

Reasons: _____

_____

Work in small groups. Talk about each of the previous problems and decide what your group would do. Try to use some of the words and phrases about family on page 82.

FROM THE NEWS

Preparing to Read

Answer the questions before you read. Discuss your answers as a class.

1. Under what circumstances is it a good idea for adult children to live at home with their parents?

2. What are some of the social and economic reasons that adult children return home to live?

3. Is it acceptable in your culture for adult children to live with their families? Why?

4. What are some possible problems with adult children returning to their parents' homes to live?

Boomerang Kids Don't Have to Be a Financial Drain

Establishing Ground Rules Makes all the Difference

ENGLEWOOD, COLORADO—A few years ago, a great deal of publicity focused on the difficulties parents face in adjusting to life after their children leave home. These days, however, the situation is reversed. Empty-nest syndrome[1] has given way to the trend of "boomerang kids,"[2] who are moving back in with Mom and/or Dad more than ever before. This **trend** affects more than daily routines. The financial burden of children moving back home can be significant.

However, "boomerang kids" don't have to cause money-related **turmoil.** According to William L. Anthes, Ph.D., president and CEO of the National Endowment for Financial Education® (NEFE®), some advance discussion and planning can help ensure a positive experience for the entire household.

WHO IS LIKELY TO BOOMERANG

The latest U.S. census showed that in 2000, with the nation's economy sliding, more than 25 percent of Americans between the ages of 18 and 34 were living with their parents. For those aged 18 to 24, the numbers were even higher; 56 percent of men and 43 percent of women were living with one or both parents. "If the economy doesn't soon improve, this phenomenon is likely to increase," Anthes says. A recent survey taken by Monstertrak.com, an online source of jobs and employment information, found that 60 percent of college students said they planned to move back in with their parents after graduation.

While every family's situation is unique, most adult children who move in with their parents share similar **traits.** Boomerang kids have been on their own in the world for a period of time, and they have decided to move home temporarily. Their reasons for returning home run the gamut from job loss to divorce—but financial problems usually are the underlying motivation.

HOW TO ESTABLISH LIMITS

"Most parents will do anything in their power to help their children through a difficult time. But they shouldn't do so to the **detriment** of their own financial well-being. Parents need to focus on saving and planning for their upcoming retirement, and they should not lose sight of this goal," Anthes says. However, establishing a plan that sets limits may avoid **potential** problems and help ensure a smooth-running home.

SET THE GROUND RULES

Begin by discussing your basic requirements with your boomerang kid. "Let your child know that things will be different in your home this time around," Anthes says. "Having been independent, your child is now an adult and should have all the responsibilities that go along with that **status.** Unless you make this clear, your son or daughter is likely to fall back into the comfortable role of the **nurtured** child."

Anthes encourages parents to come up with a list of basic ground rules. "These should be non-negotiable terms for living in the family home. Include specific standards for things like noise, smoking, alcohol and visitors. Use common sense in outlining all the points that could cause conflict later. As you make them clear to your child, also emphasize the **consequences** for breaking these rules."

In most cases the ground rules should include a **tentative** limit on the length of time the child may remain in the home. "Some situations may require an open-ended or extended stay, but such considerations are rare. Usually, it is best to clarify how long the arrangement will last," Anthes says.

NEGOTIATE THE ASSIGNMENT OF SPECIFIC RESPONSIBILITIES

Anthes encourages parents to focus on two categories: financial contributions and household chores.

Although circumstances will vary with each family, a discussion of finances and household chores may include responsibility for rent, food, cleaning, and laundry.

---

[1]*empty nest syndrome:* a situation in which parents become sad because their children have grown up and moved out of the house

[2]*boomerang kids:* adult children who have left home but return to live with their parents

WHAT MAKES A HAPPY HOME

"Boomerang kids, while they bring with them the potential for emotional and financial stress, also can have a positive impact on the household," Anthes says. "Many parents enjoy the company of their adult children and are pleased to have them back, especially if they take on extra responsibilities."

"Families are amazingly **resilient**," Anthes says. "They pull together to provide emotional and financial support when it is needed. Boomerang kids may need a little or a lot of help, depending on their situation, but the best approach in virtually all cases is to set standards and establish a plan that moves them back to independence as soon as possible."

Checking Your Comprehension

Scan the news article for the answers to these questions, and write your responses.

1. What traits do most boomerang kids share? _____

   _____

2. Why should parents have a plan? _____

   _____

3. What should be included in the ground rules? Describe some general and specific items. _____

   _____

4. What should parents' ultimate goal be for their boomerang kids?

   _____

Thinking Critically About the Reading

Discuss these topics in small groups. Then share your responses with the class.

1. Why do parents sometimes have to protect themselves from boomerang kids? If you know of actual examples, describe one.

2. What positive effects can boomerang kids have on a household? Describe some actual examples.

3. Do you agree that boomerang kids should have to contribute money and perform household chores when they move back in with their families? Why?

4. What kinds of social and economic changes might decrease the numbers of boomerang kids?

WORDS AND PHRASES FROM THE READING

Look at the words below. Find them in boldface print in the news article on pages 86–87. Look at the context of each word. Can you figure out the meaning? Match the words on the left with their meanings on the right. Use a dictionary if necessary.

1. _____ consequences
2. _____ detriment
3. _____ nurtured
4. _____ potential
5. _____ resilient
6. _____ status
7. _____ tentative
8. _____ traits
9. _____ trend
10. _____ turmoil

a. a person's social or professional rank or position

b. possible

c. harm or damage that is done to something

d. able to quickly become strong, healthy, happy again after an illness, difficult situation, change, etc.

e. not definite or certain; subject to change

f. things that happen as a result of an action or situation

g. a state of confusion, excitement, or trouble

h. well cared for; protected

i. particular qualities in someone's character; characteristics

j. a general tendency in a way a situation is changing or developing

Complete the sentences using these phrases from the reading. Use a dictionary if necessary.

fall back into	ground rules	lose sight of
open ended	pull together	run the gamut

1. Family situations vary widely; they _____ from nuclear families to extended families.

2. Whenever many people live in one household, it is important to set _____ so that everyone can contribute and get along.

3. Boomerang kids and their parents must not _____ the fact that the situation is temporary and the kids will most likely leave home soon.

4. When kids grow up, become adults, and leave home, they learn to be independent. But, if they return home to a mother who takes care of them, it's easy to _____ old habits they might have had as children.

5. To help boomerang kids regain their independence, parents should explain that the new living arrangement is not _____; the stay will be for a limited amount of time.

6. In times of trouble, families can _____ and help each other out.

CONVERSATION TIP

There will be situations in which you need to tell someone you have a made a firm decision. Here are some ways to express your determination and not let the other person change your mind.

EXPRESSING DETERMINATION
This is what I have decided to do.
I've made up my mind.
There's no talking me out of this.
I am determined to . . .
I've thought long and hard about this.
There is nothing you can say to change my mind.
It's a done deal.
I'm sticking to my guns about this.

ACT IT OUT

Act out the situation with a partner. Use the conversation tip expressions in the box and the words and phrases from the unit to act out the following role play.

Situation

You and one of your parents are having a discussion. You are twenty-one years old and have decided to move to a faraway country. Your father and mother don't want you to go. You feel that this move is important to your future and you are determined to go.

Work with one other student. Student A is the parent. Student B is the adult child who has decided to move away.

EXAMPLE

Student A: I don't think you should move so far away.

Student B: I think it is a great opportunity for me. This is what I've decided to do.

Student A: You'll be so far away. We won't see you often.

Student B: I know, but I can call often. I've thought a long time about this and I've made up my mind.

PROVERBS AND SAYINGS ABOUT FAMILY

Explore what people say and think about family ties and friendship. Read and discuss the meaning of each quotation in small groups.

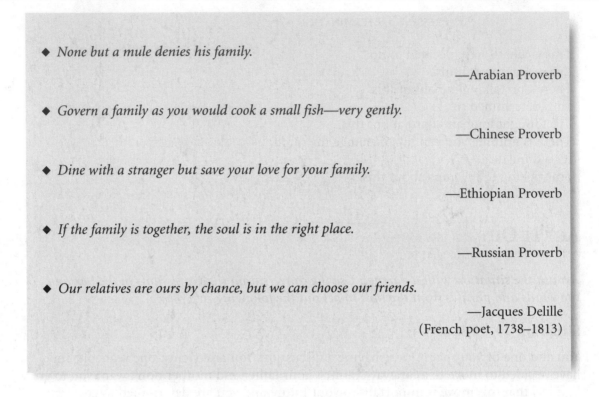

◆ *None but a mule denies his family.*

—Arabian Proverb

◆ *Govern a family as you would cook a small fish—very gently.*

—Chinese Proverb

◆ *Dine with a stranger but save your love for your family.*

—Ethiopian Proverb

◆ *If the family is together, the soul is in the right place.*

—Russian Proverb

◆ *Our relatives are ours by chance, but we can choose our friends.*

—Jacques Delille
(French poet, 1738–1813)

Work in your groups to discuss what these sayings mean to you. Which ones do you agree with? Why? Which one best describes how you feel about family? If none of them does, find one that does.

BEYOND THE CLASSROOM

In some cultures, elderly people live at home with the family. In other cultures, elderly people may live on their own or move into special homes with other elders. What are your views about who should take care of older people who need assistance? Write a short personal essay that describes your opinions about whether families should care for their older members or whether older people should live on their own or in retirement homes.

9

Information Technology— Pros and Cons

THINKING ABOUT THE TOPIC

Talk in small groups or with the whole class.

1. Which picture shows video conferencing? What is the difference between a conference call and a video conference?

2. Which picture shows people sending messages back and forth on the computer? How is this different from talking to someone in person?

3. Which picture shows someone on a cell phone? How have cell phones affected our sense of privacy? Why wasn't this true of landline phones?

TALKING ABOUT YOUR EXPERIENCE

Information technology has changed the way we interact. Now, we can send an e-mail to someone, and the person receives it almost instantaneously. With cell phones, we can reach people at any time and any place, not just at work or at home. The Internet allows us to access unlimited information without leaving our desks. New technologies may have made communication faster and easier, but have they improved how we interact with each other?

Look at the communication methods on the chart. Check off any technology that you have used. Briefly describe the advantages and disadvantages of each method of communicating.

Information Technology

Have Used	Communication Technology	Advantages	Disadvantages
	E-mail		
	Cell phone		
	Instant Messaging (IM)		
	Internet		
	Fax		

Discuss with a partner:

1. Compare the advantages and disadvantages you listed with your partner's. How were your responses similar? How were they different?

2. Have advances in communication technology made our lives harder or easier? Explain.

3. What are some of the negative aspects of each new technology? For example, e-mail is a quick, easy way of communicating, but what happens when you receive too many e-mails from friends and lots of junk e-mail?

4. Computers are capable of multitasking, doing more than one job at a time. Now workers are expected to do the same—perform many tasks at once. Is this a good trend? Explain.

LISTENING

Preparing to Listen

You are about to listen to a conversation between a mother and a father about technology and what is best for their children. Answer the questions before you listen. Discuss your answers as a class.

1. How do you think that changes in technology have affected children in particular? Explain.

2. Do you think that changes in technology have separated the generations from one another? If so, how?

Listening for Details

Look at the chart headings below. Then listen to the conversation at least twice. As you listen, write down the father's and mother's different views and opinions about technology and its effects. You do not need to write complete sentences. Just take notes.

Father's Attitude Toward Technology	Mother's Attitude Toward Technology

Responding to the Listening

Discuss the questions in small groups.

1. Do you think it is important to keep up with the latest trends in technology? Explain.

2. Do you think technologies like computers and cell phones detract from our social interaction or enhance it? Explain.

3. Do your friends have a different perspective on technology than your parents or grandparents do? Explain.

WORDS AND PHRASES ABOUT INFORMATION TECHNOLOGY

Information technology has changed the way we communicate and given birth to many new words and expressions.

Check your knowledge of computer terms. Match the words and phrases on the left with their meanings on the right. Use a dictionary if necessary.

1. _____ blog

2. _____ chat room

3. _____ computer crash

a. a humorous expression meaning letters that are sent through the mail and not by e-mail

b. the ability to do more than one job at a time

c. short for *Weblog*, a Web page that is like an informal daily journal for an individual, group, or community

4. ____ cyberspace	**d.** all the connections between computers in different places, considered as a real place where information, messages, pictures, exist
5. ____ hardware	
6. ____ multitasking	
7. ____ search engine	**e.** an occasion when a computer or computer system stops working
8. ____ software	**f.** computer equipment and machinery
9. ____ snail mail	**g.** the programs that tell a computer what to do
10. ____ spam	**h.** a computer program that helps you find information on the Internet
11. ____ surfing the Net/Web	
12. ____ virus	**i.** a place on the Internet where you can write messages to other people and receive messages back from them immediately, so that you can have a conversation

j. to use a computer to look through information on the Internet for anything that interests you

k. a set of instructions secretly put into a computer or computer program that can destroy information stored there and possibly the equipment itself

l. a computer message to many different people, usually as a way of advertising something

PROBLEM SOLVING

Read and listen to each problem. Then look at the possible solutions given and add some of your own. Decide what you would do in each case. Write the reasons for your decision.

Problem 1

You subscribe to several e-mail lists on a variety of topics. You receive an e-mail that you have a strong personal reaction to. You want to communicate directly with the sender and express your feelings. You specifically do not want to share your thoughts with the whole group. You hit "reply," compose your e-mail and send it. You suddenly realize you have sent it to the whole group, not the person. What do you do?

1. Send a follow-up e-mail to the group explaining what happened.

2. E-mail the person who you wanted to receive it and explain what happened.

3. _____

4. _____

Reasons: _____

_____

Problem 2

Although you are very busy and you do not live near your grandparents, you want to keep in touch with them. You typically use e-mail in order to communicate and also to send digital photographs. You buy your grandparents a new computer so that they can communicate easily with you. They insist they can't learn how to use it and don't want it. They would rather you just call or send snail mail. Because of your busy schedule, e-mail is a lot easier for you. What do you do?

1. Find the time to write letters and call.

2. Continue to encourage them to learn how to use e-mail.

3. _____

4. _____

Reasons: _____

_____

Problem 3

You take the train to and from work every day. It is your quiet time to read or just relax. One day you are enjoying your time reading a very good book. The person behind you is having a loud, personal conversation on a cell phone. She is talking to her friend about some very personal information that you do not want to hear. What do you do?

1. Move to another seat

2. Ask her to keep her voice down.

3. _____

4. _____

Reasons: _____

_____

Work in small groups. Talk about each of the previous problems and decide what your group would do. Try to use some of the words and phrases about computers on pages 93–94.

FROM THE NEWS

Preparing to Read

Answer the questions with a partner before you read. Discuss your answers as a class.

1. How do the older people in your family feel about new methods of communication? Why do they feel this way?

2. How might the new technologies help elderly people stay in touch with others? How might the new devices be a barrier to communication?

Retirees Ease Loneliness with Computers

By Nona Yates

Surfing the Internet is generally thought of as a young person's **pursuit,** but don't try floating that **notion** at the Leisure World retirement community in Laguna Hills, California.

"It's unbelievable how these elderly people take to computers," said Joe Schwarz, 76, president of the Leisure World PC Users Group. "It keeps them doing something interesting, keeps them from being lonely."

And lest[1] you're thinking, well, he would say that, consider the numbers: Schwarz's group boasts more than 900 members, and the community's Macintosh Users Group has more than 200 **enthusiasts.**

Computer experience **ranges** from the "just curious" with no computer background to full-fledged nerds[2] who have a computer at home, a laptop in the RV, and another computer in their second home.

"One resident (couple) has a dual setup, with 'his and hers' computers," said Norm Salzberg, 69, publicity director for the PC Users Group. Some have parlayed[3] their knowledge into lucrative[4] sidelines, including publishing newsletters and creating greeting cards and invitations for residents.

With a full complement of classes, special interest groups, a computer lab, and two learning centers, the group's teachers and officers, all volunteers, are hard-pressed to keep up with the demand.

"It's a labor of love,"[5] said Shell Weinberg, 66, who became interested in computers through the Leisure World Mac Users Group and is now manager of the Macintosh Learning Center.

Love sometimes plays a role in other ways too. Newlyweds Charles Nahas and his wife, Robin, co-teach beginning computer classes. One recently married member met his spouse when he called a computer helpline and hit it off with the technician.

Every age group is represented, from people in their fifties to several members in their nineties. Most are in their seventies and eighties, according to group officers.

These active seniors use the Internet to connect with others with common interests through SeniorNet (http://www.seniornet.org), make travel plans at the Elderhostel (http://www.elderhostel.org) site, take classes through **Virtual University** (http://www.athena.edu), get involved in political activism, or get local information from the "Electric Village," a site for residents.

GENEALOGY A BIG ATTRACTION

They communicate with their children and grandchildren by e-mail; track their retirement funds and stock portfolios with money management software; create **graphics** for posters, greeting cards and family photos; and write letters and family histories with word-processing software.

Genealogy is a big draw for many of Leisure World's computer users. Dale Gibson, 91, uses the Internet and e-mail, along with more traditional forms of communication, for a family genealogy project.

Ann Hairfield, 69, PC Users Group secretary, connects with others who have systemic lupus,[6] which she suffers from, and learns about the latest medical news via[7] the Internet and e-mail.

"I kept in touch with my granddaughter on board the USS *Theodore Roosevelt* air carrier in the Persian Gulf" said John Fuller, 76, recently, a vice president of the group. "She even sent me some photographs she took on shore leave by computer that I can download and print here."

COMPUTER WAS GIFT FOR 88TH BIRTHDAY

Ilse Wolfson, 72, a member who is visually impaired, has **enlisted** the computer as an aid to help her overcome her disability.

"I could no longer read what I had typed. (Now) I have a 17-inch screen and I can enlarge the type to whatever I need at any particular time and print it out at a regular size for others to read," she said.

Using the technology also helps to **alleviate** the **isolation** of homebound seniors.

One of the newest members joined just a month ago.

"I gave myself a computer for my 88th birthday," Isadore Markin said. "I'm a babe in the woods now."

---

[1] *lest:* for fear or worry that

[2] *nerds:* people who are extremely focused on a technical or scientific subject and may sometimes act inappropriately in social situations

[3] *parlayed:* used something to great advantage

[4] *lucrative:* profitable

[5] *labor of love:* something that is hard work but that you do because you want to very much

[6] *systemic lupus:* a disease that affects the skin and joints

[7] *via:* by way of, by using

Checking Your Comprehension

Write your responses to the following items according to the information and opinions in the news article.

1. What is the range of computer experience among members of the Leisure World retirement community?

   _____

2. How have members of the Leisure World retirement community used their computer knowledge to make money?

   _____

3. What age groups are represented at the Leisure World community?

   _____

4. What kinds of Internet sites have the seniors used?

   _____

5. How have some of the elders used computers to stay in touch with their families?

   _____

6. How has computer technology been helpful to retirees with illnesses?

   _____

Thinking Critically About the Reading

Discuss in small groups. Then share your responses with the class.

1. What surprised you about the information in the article?
2. What people in your community or family might benefit from increasing their computer skills? How would they benefit?
3. Do you think that computers can ease loneliness for users of any age? Why?
4. Why are computers particularly helpful for retirees?
5. Have you ever tried to teach an older person how to use a computer, cell phone, or other advanced technological device? If so, what was the experience like?

WORDS AND PHRASES FROM THE READING

Look at the words below. Find them in boldface print in the news article on page 96. Look at the context of each word. Can you figure out the meaning? Match the words on the left with their meanings on the right. Use a dictionary if necessary.

1. _____ alleviate
2. _____ enlisted
3. _____ enthusiasts

a. drawings or images that are designed to represent objects or facts

b. people who are very interested in a particular activity or subject

c. an idea, belief, or opinion about something, especially one that may be wrong

4. _____ genealogy

5. _____ graphics

6. _____ isolation

7. _____ notion

8. _____ pursuit

9. _____ ranges

10. _____ virtual

d. an activity, such as a hobby, that you spend a lot of time doing

e. engaged the support or help of something or someone

f. the study of the history of families

g. varies in amount within specified limits

h. relating to something made, done, or seen on a computer rather than in the real world

i. to make something less bad, painful, severe or difficult

j. being alone or unable to meet or speak to other people

Read the sentences. Circle the letter of the best definition for the underlined phrase.

1. I'd <u>be hard-pressed</u> to meet someone who has never heard of a computer. Everyone seems to know what a computer is.
   a. to have difficulty doing something
   b. to be cramped for space

2. Having brand-new computers in our language lab is a <u>big draw</u>. Everyone likes to use the latest equipment.
   a. an attraction
   b. a disadvantage

3. I'm taking a class on computer design, and my new classmates and I <u>hit it off</u> really well. I've made some nice new friends.
   a. slapped one another on the back
   b. liked one another immediately

4. I don't know what I would do without computer <u>help lines</u>. Whenever I have a problem that I need to solve, it's great to know I can call someone up for help.
   a. a phone number to call if you need advice or information
   b. a computer program you can install to prevent a virus from infecting your computer

5. I am sure once you learn to surf the Internet you will <u>take to</u> it immediately; you will like being able to find information so quickly.
   a. to need a long time to like something
   b. to start to like something or someone

CONVERSATION TIP

When you are describing how you feel about an issue, or what your perspective is on it, these phrases can help you. Use them before stating what you want to say on a subject.

GIVING YOUR PERSPECTIVE	
Formal	From my perspective . . . One way to look at it is . . . On the other hand
Informal	The way I see it is . . . Look at it this way If you ask me . . .

ACT IT OUT

Work in small groups. Use the conversation tip expressions in the box and the words and phrases from the unit to discuss the following situations. One student plays the role of the discussion leader. The others are active participants, and each person must have at least one turn to express his or her perspective on the situation.

Situations

- Children who spend a lot of time online using IM
- Students who use online essays, slightly alter them, and turn them in for school assignments
- Teens who spend hours on end playing games on the computer
- People who spend hours talking to friends on their cell phone
- People who send spam e-mail
- People who create computer viruses

> **EXAMPLE**
>
> ***Discussion Leader:*** *What do you think about children who spend a lot of time online using IM?*
>
> ***Student A:*** *If you ask me, children spend way too much time online. I think they should be outside playing with friends.*
>
> ***Student B:*** *The way I see it is, kids are using the computer, but they are writing to each other. They are practicing their language skills.*
>
> ***Student C:*** *From my perspective, children need more face-to-face interaction.*

SAYINGS ABOUT TECHNOLOGICAL PROGRESS

What have people said about technology? Read and discuss the meaning of each quotation in small groups.

◆ *Technological progress has merely provided us with more efficient means for going backwards.*

—Aldous Huxley
(English critic and novelist, 1894–1963)

◆ *Any sufficiently advanced technology is indistinguishable from magic.*

—"Clarke's Third Law," Arthur C. Clarke
(British author and inventor, b. 1917)

◆ *If it keeps up, man will atrophy all his limbs but the push-button finger.*

—Frank Lloyd Wright
(American architect, 1867–1959)

◆ *It has become appallingly obvious that our technology has exceeded our humanity.*

—Albert Einstein
(German-born physicist, 1879–1955)

◆ *We've arranged a civilization in which most crucial elements profoundly depend on science and technology.*

—Carl Sagan
(author and astronomer, 1934–1996)

◆ *You go to your TV to turn your brain off. You go to the computer when you want to turn your brain on.*

—Steve Jobs
(Apple Computer CEO, b. 1955)

Some of these quotes about technology pre-date the Information Age. Discuss the following questions with your group:

- How were people able to predict the effects of technology accurately before it existed?
- Why are many people critical of technology?
- What kinds of technological changes do you foresee fifty years from now?

BEYOND THE CLASSROOM

Continue to explore the unit theme by completing the following activities.

1. Imagine that all forms of communication you learned about in this unit (the Internet, e-mail, cell phones) have disappeared. What would your life be like? Write a diary entry in which you describe a typical day without the use of a computer, e-mail, a cell phone, or any other new electronic device.

2. Spam has become a large problem for e-mail users. Use the Internet to research laws on spam and what is being done to curtail it. Present your findings to the class.

10

A Good Place to Work

THINKING ABOUT THE TOPIC

Talk in small groups or with the whole class.

1. Describe each item on the list and why it is important.

2. Under what circumstances are some items more important than others?

3. Is one item most important? Why?

TALKING ABOUT YOUR EXPERIENCE

People often work at a particular job out of necessity. They have to make enough money to support themselves and their families. In an ideal world, people would have the luxury of choosing a work situation that was well-suited to their personal needs and values. If you had the time and money to choose an ideal job, what type of company would you want to work for?

Which of the following would you consider when deciding on the ideal workplace for you? Rank each item from 1 to 10, with 1 being the most important and 10 being the least important.

7 _1_ High salary

3 _10_ A location close to home

2 _1_ Good health insurance benefits

6 _10_ Pension plans and tax-saving retirement accounts

9 _1_ On-the-job training and financial help with continuing education

4 _10_ Flexible work hours; optional overtime

5 _1_ Job security—few layoffs and company loyalty to long-term workers

8 _1_ The opportunity to move up within the company

1 _10_ A workplace that coincides with your personal values

10 _10_ A company that donates money or service to the community

Discuss with a partner.

1. How were you and your partner's ideal job situations similar? How were they different? Describe why you ranked the items the way you did.

2. Why are health care benefits so important to most workers?

3. Why do people leave a job when they are earning a lot of money and are not asked to leave?

4. Do you think that profitable companies should give money back to the community in some way? Why?

LISTENING

Preparing to Listen

You are about to listen to an informational interview. During this type of interview, a person who is interested in a particular company or career will contact the company to find out general information about it and to see if it is a good place to work. There are many kinds of informational interviews. The one you are about to hear is quite informal. Respond to the following before you listen.

What sort of questions would you want to ask during an informational interview? Write down three questions you might ask.

1. _____

2. _____

3. _____

Listening for Details

Read the statements below. Then listen to the conversation at least twice. As you listen, mark the statements as true (T) or false (F) according to the information and opinions in the article. If a statement is false, correct it to make it true.

1. __F__ Yolanda is looking for a job as a marketing director.

2. __F__ Melinda used to work in Los Angeles.

3. __F__ Yolanda thinks that Allied's salaries for marketing assistants are competitive.

4. __T__ Yolanda is a working mother.

5. __T__ Allied Industries offers generous health and education benefits.

6. __T__ Yolanda thinks that the company's daycare facility is a great company benefit.

7. __T__ Yolanda is disappointed about Allied's vacation policies.

8. __F__ This year, Allied is giving part of its profits to the local high school.

Responding to the Listening

Discuss the questions in small groups.

1. How were Yolanda's questions similar to or different from the three questions you wrote in Preparing to Listen, above? Is there some question Yolanda didn't ask that you would like to have asked?

2. Should Yolanda have brought up salary during an informational interview? Why?

3. Would you be interested in working at a place like Allied Industries? Why?

4. Does it matter to you whether the company you work for donates some of its profits to worthy causes? Why?

5. How would you describe the head of Allied Industries?

WORDS AND PHRASES ABOUT BUSINESS

Work with a partner. Match the words and phrases on the left with their definitions on the right. Write the letter on the line. Use a dictionary if necessary.

1. __c__ multinational corporation
2. __e__ public company
3. __b__ charitable foundation
4. __d__ cooperative
5. __a__ mom-and-pop

    a. an informal term for a small business owned and operated by a family or a husband and wife

    b. an organization that gives or collects money or gifts to be used to help people in need

    c. a big company, or group of companies, which has offices, factories, etc., in many countries

    d. an organization, such as a company or factory, in which all the employees own an equal share of the business

    e. a company that offers its stock for sale to people who are not part of the company

Work with a partner. Use the words and phrases about business to complete the sentences.

1. During high school, I worked as a waitress at a __mom-and-pop__ restaurant run by the family next door.

2. Levi Strauss is a __multinational corporation__, with stores in countries all over the world.

3. Apple is a __public company__; its stock is for sale to people outside the company.

4. My sister works at an organic food __cooperative__ and receives a share of the produce in addition to her salary.

5. Ben & Jerry's Foundation is a non-profit, __charitable foundation__ that funds projects to solve societal and environment problems.

Match the abbreviations on the left with the words they stand for on the right. Then use a dictionary to look up the meaning of each abbreviation.

1. __c__ CEO
2. __e__ HR
3. __b__ HMO
4. __a__ EEO
5. __d__ PPO

    a. Equal Employment Opportunity

    b. Health Maintenance Organization

    c. Chief Executive Officer

    d. Preferred Provider Organization

    e. Human Resources

PROBLEM SOLVING

Read and listen to each problem. Then look at the possible solutions given and add one or two of your own. Decide what you would do in each case. Write the reasons for your decision.

Problem 1

You work for a pharmaceutical company, testing new medications. In a recent test, you noticed problems with a small percentage of people taking a new drug. Your boss said you should ignore the problem. You feel uncomfortable about the situation. What do you do?

1. Speak to your boss's boss.

2. Don't say anything because it only affects a small percentage of people.

3. _____

4. _____

Reasons: _____

_____

Problem 2

One of your job responsibilities is to recruit new employees. Your boss recently asked you to find the best candidate for a position, but to keep the search confidential. Your friend has that job now. You now realize your friend is about to be replaced. What do you do?

1. Warn your friend that the company might be in the process of replacing her.

2. Do your job and keep your mouth shut.

3. _____

4. _____

Reasons: _____

_____

Problem 3

You work for a large company and love your job. You recently learned that the company discriminates against older employees. They are laid off more often than younger employees, but are told the company is "reducing its workforce." You have seen the company fire elderly workers and then hire younger ones. What do you do?

1. Continue working at the company and say nothing since you like your job.

2. Secretly encourage the people who are laid off to fight back.

3. _____

4. _____

Reasons: _____

_____

Work in small groups. Talk about each of the previous problems and decide what your group would do. Try to use some of the words and phrases about business on pages 104–105.

Preparing to Read

Answer the questions before you read. Discuss your answers as a class.

1. Businesses exist to make money. Why do some companies do things to help the environment or improve working conditions?

2. Do you know any companies that help the environment or do other good deeds? Which ones?

3. If you found out that a company was donating money to a cause you believed in, would you be more likely to buy its products? Explain.

IKEA in the News

By David Selley

Most Canadians have heard of IKEA, the world's largest furniture retailer.[1] Many have shopped there because of the quality of the products, comparatively low prices, bright, attractive, and "fun" surroundings (children's ball room and first-rate cafeteria, for example), all in spite of jammed parking lots and sometimes long line-ups at the cashiers. On October 9, 1999, IKEA conducted a well-publicized event in which the entire day's **gross** sales were divided among its employees. Shoppers worldwide flocked to IKEA and revenues for the day were $118 million, shared among over 40,000 employees. The previous record day's sales were $65 million!

IKEA was in the news again in November when it announced an agreement with its worldwide solid wood suppliers, including those in British Columbia, whereby all suppliers will **guarantee** that the wood does not **originate** in ancient forests.

IKEA is a hugely successful multinational company owned by a Netherlands charitable foundation. It has revenues[2] of about $11 billion; almost 200 million people a year visit its stores. Since it is not a public company, IKEA chooses not to reveal detailed financial data.

The company was founded in Sweden in the nineteen forties by Ingvar Kamprad, who is still the primary motivator of IKEA's **vision** and the **instigator** of the October 9 event, according to Ms. Laurence Martocq, IKEA Canada's Director of Public Relations. "Home furnishings that combine good design, good function, and good quality with prices so low that as many people as possible can afford them," and "creating a better everyday life for the majority of people" were, and still are, Mr. Kamprad's (and IKEA's) goal. As well, Ms. Martocq says that **collegiality** and trust among all employees (who are called "co-workers") is also a secret of the company's success.

From the beginning, Mr. Kamprad has focused on ethical issues. IKEA has forged alliances with Greenpeace on environmental matters and with UNICEF, Save The Children and similar interest groups. Marianne Barner, IKEA's ombudsman[3] for children, works in IKEA's International Headquarters in Denmark. Ms. Barner says her responsibility is the human rights and best interests of children and to ensure that IKEA's operations improve, not worsen, the lot of children. IKEA conducts inspections of its suppliers'[4] operations and Ms. Barner says she is encouraged in recent years by a much greater supplier awareness of the child labor issue. Ms. Martocq provided a further example of the company's concern for its suppliers' workers. IKEA took the CEOs and one other **executive** from each of the 28 countries in which it has stores on a tour of supplier **operations** in India so that they could see for themselves the conditions under which their goods were produced.

A number of interesting corporate ethics issues are raised by IKEA's business success and focus on ethical issues:

• To what extent is the ethical conduct a contributor to business success, and what does it cost? The October 9 event "cost"

IKEA $118 million in the short run, probably much more because of the cost of organizing and running the event. The long run payback may well be enormous, but likely immeasurable. Perhaps it resulted from purely altruistic[5] **motives.**

- Does the fact that IKEA is not obligated to meet shareholder expectations on a quarterly basis give it a special advantage? If so, what does that say about the **shareholder** model that most multinational businesses must operate in? Should we be encouraging alternatives to the shareholder model—the cooperative movement, for example?

- IKEA's priorities appear to be customers and potential customers, "co-workers," supplier working conditions, the environment, and "people" generally. If shareholders are added to the list (usually at the top), do the other priorities have to suffer? How can a clear link be established between ethical conduct and business success even when shareholder demands have to be met?

---

[1] *retailer:* a store that sells goods

[2] *revenues:* money that a business or organization receives over a period of time, especially from selling goods or services

[3] *ombudsman:* someone who deals with complaints made by people against a company, the government, etc.

[4] *suppliers:* companies that provide a particular product

[5] *altruistic:* thinking of the needs and desires of other people instead of your own

Checking Your Comprehension

Write your responses to the following items according to the information and opinions in the news article.

1. What did IKEA do on October 9, 1999?

_____

2. How much money was divided among the 40,000 employees of IKEA?

_____

3. What agreement did IKEA make with solid wood suppliers?

_____

4. What are some goals of IKEA and its founder, Ingvar Kamprad?

_____

5. How has IKEA shown concern for the interest of children?

_____

6. Why did IKEA's CEO and other executives travel to India?

_____

Thinking Critically About the Reading

Discuss in small groups. Then share your responses with the class.

1. Why do you think IKEA chose to give gross sales back to employees on October 9, 1999?

2. IKEA is concerned about working conditions and the environment. What do you think motivates this concern?

3. IKEA is not a public company, so it does not have to share its financial information. Do you think IKEA would behave differently if it had to share such information? Why?

4. Would you consider working for IKEA? Why?

5. Do you want to shop at IKEA now that you have read this article? Why?

WORDS AND PHRASES FROM THE READING

Look at the words below. Find them in boldface print in the news article on pages 107–108. Look at the context of each word. Can you figure out the meaning? Match the words on the left with their meanings on the right. Use a dictionary if necessary.

1. __g__ collegiality
2. __f__ executive
3. __a__ gross
4. __i__ guarantee
5. __d__ instigator
6. __h__ motives
7. __j__ operations
8. __c__ originate
9. __e__ shareholder
10. __b__ vision

a. total profit before taxes have been deducted

b. an idea of what you think something should be like

c. to start in a particular place; to come into being

d. someone who starts something such as a new policy or legal process

e. someone who owns stock in a business; stockholder

f. someone who manages others in an organization and helps decide what the organization will do

g. equally shared power and authority among people who work together

h. reasons that make someone do something

i. to promise that something will happen or be done

j. businesses, companies, or organizations

Read the sentences. Circle the letter of the best definition for each underlined phrase.

1. Some companies demonstrate <u>ethical conduct</u> by giving charitable contributions to other organizations. It is not something a company is required to do, but companies do it because they see it as the right thing to do.
   a. morally good or correct behavior
   b. corporate communications about right and wrong

2. IKEA has <u>forged alliances</u> with organizations in order to help the environment and develop better working conditions for children worldwide.
   a. illegally copied financial agreements
   b. developed strong relationships with other people, groups, or countries

3. IKEA has sought out organizations that focus on specific <u>interest groups</u> like those who work with children and the environment.
   a. groups of people who join together to try to influence the government in order to protect their own particular rights, advantages, concerns, etc.
   b. groups of people who share common tastes in art, music, etc.

INTERVIEWING TIPS

Before you go to a job interview, it is recommended that you review a list of *dos* and *don'ts* and anticipate the questions you are likely to be asked. This way, you won't be caught off guard and will be able to do well on the interview.

Look over the list of dos *and* don'ts. *Discuss the points in small groups.*

Interviewing *Dos* and *Don'ts*

Do	Don't
Be brief and to the point	Ramble or talk too much
Describe experiences positively	Blame past employers or criticize others
Turn weaknesses into strengths	Dwell on weakness, saying too much
Ask for clarification of vague questions	Guess at a meaning, or fake a response
Be courteous	Interrupt
Mention specific skills and experiences	Expect the résumé to speak for you
Support statements with examples	Answer just "yes" or "no"
Remember the question while answering	Ramble, then ask, "What was the question?"
Be active, involved, and enthusiastic, and ask questions	Be passive or boring
Find out when the company will make the decision and notify candidates, and follow up accordingly	Sit around waiting for a call

Below are some questions you could be asked in a job interview. Work in your groups to brainstorm possible answers to the questions.

TYPICAL INTERVIEW QUESTIONS
Tell us a little about yourself.
Why are you interested in working for this company?
What has been your greatest accomplishment?
Describe your greatest strengths and weaknesses.
What did you like best and least about your previous job?
Give an example of a problem you faced on the job, and how you solved it.
Describe a time when you were faced with problems or stressful situations at work.
What did you do to improve the situation?
What would you like to be doing five years from now?
Would you rather be in charge of a project or work as part of a team?
What have you learned from the jobs you have held?

ACT IT OUT

Act out the situation with a partner. Use the interviewing tips in the box and the words and phrases from the unit to act out the following role play.

Situation

Student A: You are preparing for a job interview. Imagine a job you would like to interview for. Write down the type of position and the kind of company. Also, prepare a list of your previous jobs, your skills, and your goals. Finally, think about how you would like to answer the questions in the interviewing tips section.

Student B: You are going to interview your partner. Read over your partner's job history and career goals. Use the interview questions above and some questions of your own to find out whether Student A is right for the job.

After you and your partner complete one interview, switch roles and do another interview.

Proverbs and Sayings About Business

What have people said about business ethics? Read and discuss the meaning of each quotation in small groups.

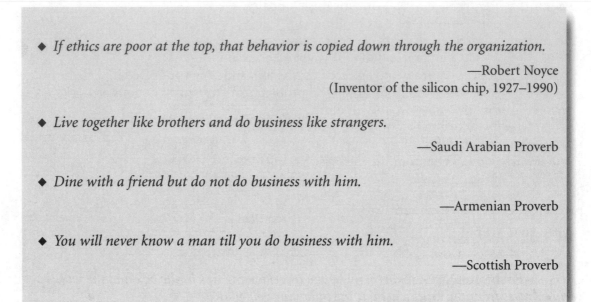

◆ *If ethics are poor at the top, that behavior is copied down through the organization.*

—Robert Noyce
(Inventor of the silicon chip, 1927–1990)

◆ *Live together like brothers and do business like strangers.*

—Saudi Arabian Proverb

◆ *Dine with a friend but do not do business with him.*

—Armenian Proverb

◆ *You will never know a man till you do business with him.*

—Scottish Proverb

Discuss with group members what the sayings reveal about our attitudes toward the business world. Do they offer a positive or a negative view of businesses and the people who work in them? Explain. Do you agree with this attitude? Why? Think of proverbs or sayings about business ethics from other cultures. What do they reveal about attitudes toward the business world?

Beyond the Classroom

Continue to explore the unit theme by completing the following activities.

1. Do Internet research on a company that invests a percentage of its profits to improve the public good, such as Ben and Jerry's, Working Assets, IKEA, and Newman's Own, Inc. Find out about the company's ethical mission, products, business practices, and charitable contributions. Write a short report on your findings and share it with the class.

2. Imagine that you are the CEO of a medium-sized company. Describe six to ten benefits you would offer your employees and explain why you believe these benefits are important to create a "good workplace." Present your benefits and ideas orally to the class. Discuss with your classmates the benefits that appealed to you most.

11

Is It the Best Medicine?

THINKING ABOUT THE TOPIC

Talk in small groups or with the whole class.

1. Which of the tests above have you had or would you be willing to have?
2. What kind of information does each test reveal?
3. Do you think that tests like these are usually reliable or not? Explain.
4. How might you feel if one of these tests revealed a health risk or a medical problem?

TALKING ABOUT YOUR EXPERIENCE

In the twenty-first century, medical technology allows us to change our appearance (plastic surgery) and detect diseases we might not know we had. Some of the new tests and procedures can improve people's mental and physical well-being, while others may actually cause more harm than good. Should people undergo procedures or tests just because they are available?

Imagine that you could change the natural course of your life through the use of advanced medical technology; for example, change the way you look or think or determine the gender of your child. What would you want to change or determine if you could? Put a check in the column that represents your answer. Add two items of your own to the chart.

I would Undergo a Test or Procedure To . . .	Yes	No	Not Sure	Reason
1. permanently change the color of my hair or eyes				
2. make sure I had a baby of the sex I wanted				
3. make me tall				
4. make me never get sick				
5. let me know what diseases I might have in the future				
6. test my unborn baby for potential diseases or disabilities				
7. _____				
8. _____				

Discuss with a partner.

1. Choose one item that you and your partner responded to differently. Why did you react the way you did? Explain your thinking to your partner.

2. In what ways might some of the tests and procedures on the chart cause problems?

3. Are any tests and procedures like these available now? Explain. Do you think that they will be available in the future? Why?

LISTENING

Preparing to Listen

You are going to listen to a conversation about a controversial medical test. Answer the questions before you listen. Discuss your answers as a class.

1. Why are some people eager to find out about a potential health problem even though they are feeling fine?

2. Why might some medical tests be dangerous to a person's physical well-being?

3. Why is it often stressful to wait for and receive medical test results?

Listening for Details

Look over the questions. Then listen to the conversation at least twice. As you listen, write down your answers to the questions. You do not need to write complete sentences. Just take notes.

1. What procedure does Mr. Lansing want to find out about?

   _____

2. Who pays for the procedure—the patient or an insurance company?

   _____

3. What is the test like?

   _____

4. How much does the procedure cost?

   _____

5. Why would Mr. Lansing want to have the procedure?

   _____

6. According to Dr. Alvarez, what happens during the procedure that could be unhealthy for the patient?

   _____

7. What kinds of problems does the procedure often find?

   _____

8. What is a "false positive"?

   _____

9. Why might the procedure lead to unnecessary or harmful surgery?

   _____

10. What alternative does Dr. Alvarez suggest for assessing a person's overall health?

    _____

Responding to the Listening

Discuss the questions in small groups.

1. What are the risks and benefits of having a full body scan?

2. In your opinion, do the benefits outweigh the risks? Explain.

3. What would you do if you had a full body scan and something potentially dangerous to your health showed up on the scan?

WORDS AND PHRASES ABOUT MEDICINE

Work with a partner to complete the sentences using the words and phrases from the box. Use a dictionary if necessary.

condition	diagnosed	prescription	procedure	specialist	symptoms

1. I am not feeling well; I have the following _____: a headache, a cough and a sore throat.

2. My mother and grandmother both had heart valve problems. I am going to get tested to see if I have the same _____.

3. Today, many nearsighted people can improve their vision by undergoing a relatively painless surgical _____.

4. My doctor just gave me a _____ for a new asthma medication.

5. My father's diabetes was _____ by our family doctor.

6. Often a general practitioner will recommend that a patient see a _____, such as an ophthalmologist, cardiologist, or dermatologist.

Work with a partner. Match the expressions on the left with their definitions on the right. Write the letter on the line. Use a dictionary if necessary.

1. ____ prone to

2. ____ under the weather

3. ____ a touch of

4. ____ side effects

a. a very small amount of something

b. feeling slightly sick

c. effects that a drug has on your body in addition to curing pain or illness

d. likely to do something or suffer from something, especially something bad or harmful

Often when a patient calls a doctor's office, the patient will speak to a nurse to determine what kind of care the patient needs before the nurse schedules an appointment. Work with a partner. Below is a conversation between a patient and a nurse in a doctor's office. Use the words and phrases about medicine to complete the conversation. When you are done, practice reading aloud the dialogue with your partner.

Nurse: What has been going on? I understand that you have not been feeling well.

Patient: Yes, I have been feeling (1) _____.

Nurse: What is wrong?

Patient: I'm not sure. I think I might have (2) _____ something, but I don't know what.

Nurse: Tell me a little bit about your (3) _____; what exactly have you been feeling?

Patient: Well, yesterday, I picked up a new (4) _____ at the drug store in the morning. I took it when I got home and within a few hours I was feeling a bit sick to my stomach. I also developed a rash.

Nurse: Why were you taking the medication?

Patient: I found out about a year ago that I had a skin disorder. It's a (5) _____ that runs in my family. I decided to undergo the recommended surgery for it about a month ago.

Nurse: So you were (6) _____ with a skin problem a year ago, had a (7) _____, and have been taking medication since then. Let's see. Oh yes, here it is in your chart. So, have you ever felt like this before, or is this the first time?

Patient: Well, I am (8) _____ stomach upsets and viruses. I'll get sick a few times each year, but this is different. I haven't felt like this before. And the rash is something new.

Nurse: OK. You could be having (9) _____ from the new medication. I think you should come in and see Dr. Lombardo, the skin (10) _____. Can you make it this afternoon at 4?

Patient: Sounds good. See you then.

PROBLEM SOLVING

Read and listen to each problem. Then look at the possible solutions given and add one or two of your own. Decide what you would do in each case. Write the reasons for your decision.

Problem 1

A friend of yours is suffering from a sudden paralysis in her arm. When she went to a traditional Western doctor, he said that she might have a brain tumor. He advised her to undergo a series of expensive tests. Your friend refuses to undergo the tests because she is very suspicious of Western medicine. She tells you that she plans to seek the help of someone who practices traditional Chinese medicine, including acupuncture and herbal remedies. What do you do?

1. Advise her to take the tests the doctor recommended.

2. Encourage her to try the traditional Chinese remedies before taking the tests.

3. _____

4. _____

Reasons: _____

_____

Problem 2

You have just been diagnosed with a rare disease. You have seen two doctors and they both said that if surgically treated, you would have roughly a 50 percent chance of being cured. However, the surgical procedure is risky and could lead to other medical problems and, in a few cases, death. Because the disease is so rare, there is very little data available about what might happen if it is left untreated. Your doctor says that if the disease progresses to a certain point, surgical treatment would no longer be possible. You are in your late forties and you have a spouse and two children. What do you do?

1. Undergo the surgical treatment despite the risks.

2. Do some more research on the disease, and get a second opinion.

3. _____

4. _____

Reasons: _____

_____

Your mother was given a drug that has just been removed from the market. Research revealed that the drug can increase the chances of heart attack and stroke by 20 percent in certain people. While your mother was taking the drug, she suffered a mini-stroke, which might have been caused by the drug. She has recovered most of her abilities, but still suffers some negative effects from the stroke and can only work part-time. A friend of yours suggests that your mother file a lawsuit against the doctor who prescribed the medication and the drug company that sold the drug. Your mother is reluctant to go to a lawyer or go through a trial. What do you do?

1. Encourage her to go to a lawyer just to get information before making her decision.

2. Encourage her to file a suit and assure her you will support her along the way.

3. _____

4. _____

Reasons: _____

_____

Work in small groups. Talk about each of the previous problems and decide what your group would do. Try to use some of the words and phrases about medicine on page 116.

FROM THE NEWS

Preparing to Read

Answer the questions before you read. Discuss your answers as a class.

1. Neurologists study and treat people who have diseases of the nerves, brain, and spinal cord. What would you think if neurologists began to help perfectly healthy people improve their intelligence and memory or change their personality traits? Would this be a good idea? Why?

2. Do you think that people should have cosmetic surgery to improve their appearance after suffering a disfiguring injury? Do you feel differently about people who undergo plastic surgery solely because they want to look younger or more attractive? Why?

Drugs Gain Attention as a Boost to Brain Power

It's called cosmetic neurology. The use of elective drugs to enhance the functioning of normal brains is gaining acceptance.

By Laura Beil

In the future, reality shows may have names such as *Extreme Makeover: Brain Edition* or *Sharp Eye for the Dumb Guy.*

At the beginning of each episode, viewers could learn about one hapless[1] soul's lifelong struggles with algebra and another's desire to not be a worrywart.[2] By the end of the hour, the transformed contestants would be winning chess matches and prancing carefree through fields of daisies. Don't check the TV listings just yet, but the idea is not all fantasy.

Some neurologists have wondered recently whether their field is the next frontier in **elective** medicine. The specialty now tries to protect ailing brains from conditions such as Parkinson's disease[3] or migraine[4] headaches. But doctors' efforts may one day extend to normal brains.

"This is coming, and we need to know it's coming," says Dr. Anjan Chatterjee of the University of Pennsylvania.

There's even a name for the field: cosmetic neurology.

As Chatterjee envisions it, cosmetic neurology could one day mean not just sharpening intelligence, but also elevating other aspects of brain function—**reflexes,** attention, mood, and memory. Studying for the SAT? Take this drug to retain more of those pesky[5] facts. About to report for duty at the fire station? These pills will improve your reflexes. Here's the 800 number. Ask your doctor.

These are not just theoretical musings. Last month in the journal *Neurology,* Dr. Chatterjee pointed out that drugs already exist that may have many of these effects. In one study, for example, emergency room patients given a memory-altering drug appeared to be **spared** some symptoms of post-traumatic stress.[6] Another small study of pilots in flight simulators suggested that those taking Alzheimer's disease[7] medications performed better, particularly under emergency conditions.

Dr. Chatterjee reserves opinion but says the idea speaks to the basic purpose of medical practice.

"I'm not arguing that this is a bad thing, and I'm not arguing it's a good thing." Before doctors are caught by surprise, he says, they need to be prepared. "What I'm hoping to do with this is get people talking."

They are. Since the journal's publication, he has fielded[8] steady e-mails. Some neurologists say they've already had patients asking about such medications for the mind.

Not all of Dr. Chatterjee's colleagues, though, agree that cosmetic neurology is **inevitable,** even if mind-improving drugs become safe and available. "There are certainly pressures that are going to push us that way," says Dr. Richard Dees of the University of Rochester. Doctors have the power, however, to shape the future of their profession regardless.

Writing in the journal, Dr. Dees argues "as neurologists and as citizens, we can collectively control our own destinies, if we choose and if we have the will to act."

Another of his colleagues has a different take.[9] Dr. Stephen Hauser of the University of California, San Francisco, wrote that "advances in neuroscience carry with them the likelihood, intended or otherwise, of medical applications that go well beyond the traditional goals to prevent, diagnose, and treat disease."

Few specialists know this as well as plastic surgeons. Before there was *Nip/Tuck*[10] and Michael Jackson's nose, plastic surgeons were rebuilding war-mangled bodies. As safety improved and public demand for cosmetic surgery grew, so did the number of cosmetic surgeons.

"You've always had a **dilemma** and a schism,"[11] says Dr. Robert Goldwyn, who has edited the *Journal of Plastic and Reconstructive Surgery,* the field's premier journal, for a quarter-century. In fact, some plastic surgeons now wonder whether their profession—under financial and public pressures—leans too far toward cosmetic surgery. And he has these words of caution for his colleagues who concentrate on the brain: "The minute technology comes along, it will be used," he says. "If doctors won't do it, other people will do it."

There are other instances of doctor-provided enhancements beyond plastic surgery, says Thomas Murray, president of The Hastings Center, a Garrison, N.Y.-based bioethics[12] research institute. Synthetic growth hormone was originally developed to help children with severe hormone **deficiencies.** But some parents have asked doctors to give it because their children are simply at the low end of the range for normal height. In response, endocrinologists[13] have tried to develop strict guidelines for its use.

"The thing about surgical enhancement is we think we can more or less understand the risks," Dr. Murray says. "With drugs it gets more complicated."

Mental enhancement with drugs is not itself unethical, he says—a cup of coffee, after all, heightens alertness beyond a natural state. Few people object to caffeine, however, because it is considered safe, is inexpensive, and is available to almost everyone.

But other drugs might not be so clear. "There are major safety concerns," Dr. Murray says. For example, someone's personality is a blend of all traits, yet no one knows whether a drug that **distorts** one mental function would **diminish** another.

In his editorial, Dr. Chatterjee also raised questions about whether cosmetic neurology might lead to **coercion** in certain professions. If a drug improved the emergency reaction of pilots, would they then be forced to take it? Would you pay more for a flight knowing the pilots took the drug?

These and other questions are those that neurologists should be asking themselves now, Dr. Murray says, before reality, if not reality television, takes them by surprise. The growth hormone story, he says, demonstrates that physicians can set standards, regardless of where public **momentum** pushes them.

Dr. Murray applauds the neurologists for raising the issue. "It alerts the profession that it needs to think about it."

[1] *hapless:* unlucky
[2] *worrywart:* someone who worries all the time
[3] *Parkinson's disease:* a serious illness in which muscles become very weak and the arms and legs shake
[4] *migraine:* an extremely bad headache that makes a person feel sick
[5] *pesky:* annoying and causing trouble
[6] *post-traumatic stress:* a mental illness that can develop after a very bad experience
[7] *Alzheimer's disease:* a disease that gradually destroys parts of the brain, especially in older people, so that they forget things and lose their ability to take care of themselves
[8] *fielded:* answered
[9] *take (on):* someone's opinion about a situation or idea
[10] *Nip/Tuck:* a TV drama about plastic surgeons
[11] *schism:* a disagreement that causes a split between two or more groups
[12] *bioethics:* medical ethics
[13] *endocrinologists:* scientists and medical doctors who study the glands in the body and the hormones they produce

Checking Your Comprehension

Choose the best answer according to the information and opinions in the news article.

1. What is cosmetic neurology?
   a. the use of medication to improve the functioning of normal brains
   b. the use of medication to improve the functioning of abnormal brains

2. According to Dr. Chatterjee, what aspects of brain function could be enhanced through the use of cosmetic neurology?
   a. people's sense of sight, smell, and hearing
   b. people's reflexes, attention, mood, and memory

3. What sorts of drugs are already being used to help normal brains function better?
   a. certain memory altering drugs used to treat emergency room patients and pilots
   b. certain drugs used to treat Parkinson's disease and migraine headaches

4. Why is Dr. Chatterjee expressing his thoughts about cosmetic neurology?
   a. He is trying to convince people to use cosmetic neurology.
   b. He wants people to talk about the issues surrounding the use of cosmetic neurology.

5. Why did endocrinologists develop strict guidelines for the use of synthetic growth hormone?
   a. The growth hormone caused personality changes in some children who were taking it.
   b. The doctors were afraid that parents of normal children would misuse the hormone because they wanted their children to be taller.

6. Why is caffeine a more acceptable way to improve mental alertness than other drugs?
   a. Caffeine is widely available, inexpensive, and considered safe while other drugs could have adverse effects on mental function and personality.
   b. Neurological studies have shown that caffeine is the safest, easiest way to improve mental functioning.

7. How might cosmetic neurology lead to coercion in the workplace?
   a. People with certain personality traits could be forced to take memory-altering drugs.
   b. People could be forced to take a drug because the medication improved a specific kind of mental functioning helpful on the job.

Thinking Critically About the Reading

Discuss in small groups. Then share your responses with the class.

1. In what ways might cosmetic neurology benefit society? In what ways might it be dangerous? Describe some of the examples in the article and some ideas and examples of your own.

2. Would you pay more to take a flight with a pilot who had taken mental-enhancing drugs? Why?

3. Who should set the standards on the use of cosmetic neurology—doctors, lawyers, the government, or the public? Explain your reasoning.

4. Would you be interested in taking mind-enhancing medications? If so, why and under what circumstances?

WORDS AND PHRASES FROM THE READING

Look at the words below. Find them in boldface print in the news article on pages 120–121. Look at the context of each word. Can you figure out the meaning? Match the words on the left with their meanings on the right. Use a dictionary if necessary.

1. _____ coercion
2. _____ deficiencies
3. _____ dilemma
4. _____ diminish
5. _____ distort
6. _____ elective
7. _____ inevitable
8. _____ momentum
9. _____ reflexes
10. _____ spared

a. involving choice, such as a treatment you choose to have, although you do not have to

b. to become smaller or less important, or make something do this

c. certain to happen and impossible to avoid

d. the use of threats or orders to make someone do something they do not want to do

e. saved from having to experience or do something

f. lack of things that are necessary

g. the ability to keep increasing, developing, or being more successful

h. movements your muscles make as a natural reaction to a physical stimulus

i. to change something so that it is strange or unclear

j. a situation in which a difficult choice must be made between two actions

Read the sentences. Circle the letter of the best definition for each underlined phrase.

1. Doctors need to address the ethical issues surrounding cosmetic neurology now to avoid being <u>caught by surprise</u> later.
   a. surprised or shocked because something was not expected
   b. surprised because something is so unethical

2. Cosmetic neurology could be the <u>next frontier</u> in medicine; it could revolutionize the way drugs are used in the future.
   a. place beyond the limit of what is currently known
   b. an area in the brain where information is stored

3. Doctors who are concerned about cosmetic neurology are speaking up about it; they are <u>raising the issue</u> and encouraging others to discuss it as well.
   a. bringing up the issue for discussion
   b. speaking in a loud voice about an issue

4. When doctors take an active role in determining the quality and nature of new medical technology, they <u>shape the future</u> of medicine.
   a. predict what will happen in the future
   b. influence the future and make it develop in a certain way

5. It is important to have <u>strict guidelines</u> for the use of new medical technologies. Ideally, these specific policies control how the technology is used and protect the public from dangerous uses or side effects.
   a. specific policies for people to follow
   b. control over people

6. The use of cosmetic neurology is not just a matter of <u>theoretical musings</u>; cosmetic neurology is already being used.
   a. studies being done
   b. thinking about something that could exist but does not exist

7. Some doctors offer these <u>words of caution</u>; if technology is available, doctors will use it. They want to warn people of the potential dangers of the new technology.
   a. warnings to be careful
   b. new technologies

QUESTIONS TO ASK YOUR DOCTOR BEFORE YOU HAVE SURGERY

Every year, millions of people worldwide have surgery. Most operations are not emergencies. This means you have time to ask your surgeon questions about the operation and time to decide whether to have it, and if so, when and where. As a patient, you can take an active role in your health care by asking questions and educating yourself.

Below are some questions you might ask your surgeon before nonemergency surgery. Read the questions with the class, and work together to brainstorm possible answers. Your answers can be realistic or imaginary.

1. What operation are you recommending?
2. Why do I need the surgery?
3. Can you explain the surgery to me? Will something be removed or repaired? If so, what?
4. Why is the surgery necessary?
5. Are there alternative ways to perform the surgery? If so, what are they and what are their benefits and risks?
6. What are the benefits of surgery? How long will the benefits last?
7. What are the risks of surgery?
8. What happens if I choose not to have the surgery?
9. Are you experienced in performing this surgery? Please explain.
10. How long will I stay in the hospital?
11. What kind of anesthesia will I need?
12. How long will it take me to recover?
13. How much will the surgery cost? Will my insurance company pay part or all of the expense?
14. Where can I get a second opinion?

ACT IT OUT

Act out the situation with a partner. Use the previous questions and the words and phrases from the unit to act out the following role play.

Situation

Student A: You are a patient about to have some kind of surgery. Decide on the nature of the surgical procedure. It could be an operation that you are familiar with, one that you have researched, or one that is completely made up. Write down a brief description of the surgical procedure and some questions you have about it. Allow your partner to read it. Then begin to ask your "doctor" your questions.

Student B: You are the doctor who will perform the surgery. You are going to answer your partner's questions about the procedure. Read your partner's description and questions. Write down several answers to your partner's questions before you begin the actual conversation.

After you and your partner complete one conversation, switch roles and repeat the role play.

> **Student A:** Is this type of eye surgery necessary to correct my vision?
>
> **Student B:** Yes. If you don't have the surgical procedure, you will never have 20/20 vision.
>
> **Student A:** Can you explain the surgery to me? How exactly is it done?
>
> **Student B:** I use a laser technique that is painless and requires no stitches.

PROVERBS AND SAYINGS ABOUT MEDICINE

Why do some people believe in medicine while others have grave doubts about it? Read and discuss the meaning of each quotation in small groups.

◆ *Medicine can only cure curable diseases, and then not always.*

—Chinese Proverb

◆ *Patience is often better than medicine.*

—German Proverb

◆ *Medicine sometimes snatches away health, sometimes gives it.*

—Ovid
(Roman poet, 43B.C.–A.D.17)

◆ *Don't live in a town where there are no doctors.*

—Yiddish Proverb

◆ *Advances in medicine and agriculture have saved vastly more lives than have been lost in all the wars in history.*

—Carl Sagan (Author and astronomer, 1934–1996)

Discuss with your group what the sayings mean to you. Which ones do you agree with? Why? Are doctors trusted and respected in your country? Think of a proverb or saying about medicine from your home country and share it with your group. Does it offer a positive or negative view?

BEYOND THE CLASSROOM

Research a controversial medical practice or procedure, such as gastric bypass, cosmetic surgery, the use of artificial growth hormone, or cloning. Write a short essay that describes the procedure and arguments for and against its use. Present your findings to the class, and take a class vote to decide whether or not the procedure should be used.

Cultural Heritage vs. Modernization

THINKING ABOUT THE TOPIC

Talk in small groups or with the whole class.

1. Today in many parts of the world historic sites exist side-by-side with modern buildings. Look at the photograph of the Louvre—a famous museum in Paris. Which part of the museum was built in the 1500s? Which part was built in the twentieth century? How can you tell?

2. How do you think the residents of Paris felt about the addition of the glass pyramid when it was first built? Why? Why do you think the glass pyramid has become popular with many visitors?

3. Why do individuals and groups become attached to a particular monument or site? Is the preservation of such buildings and places important? Why?

TALKING ABOUT YOUR EXPERIENCE

Think about a place that you and/or other people associate with cultural identity and the past. It could be a monument, a statue, the remains of an ancient civilization, or a natural site. For example, you might select the Forbidden City in Beijing, the Statue of Liberty in New York, the cliff dwellings of the Pueblo in Mesa Verde, or Tikal National Park in Guatemala.

Respond to the questions on a separate sheet of paper. Then share your responses with a partner.

1. What is the name of the place you chose? How do you know about this place? What is it like? Provide a detailed description.

2. In what ways does this place evoke cultural identity and/or the past?

3. What would happen if this place were changed or destroyed? Would something be lost? If so, what?

4. Could this place be improved or reproduced by modern architects and technology? If so, how? If not, why? Explain your response.

LISTENING

Preparing to Listen

You are going to listen to a reporter interview people about a new Wal-Mart store that has gone up near the ancient site of Teotihuacán in Mexico. Although the interview is imaginary, the situation is real. Answer the questions before you listen. Discuss your answers as a class.

1. What are some of the reasons why people believe in preserving their cultural heritage?

2. In what cases might modernization be more important than the preservation of an historic, cultural, or natural site? If you know of a good example, describe it.

Listening for Details

Read the headings on the chart. Listen to the interview at least twice. As you listen, fill in the information on the chart. You do not need to write complete sentences. Just take notes.

Reporter's facts about Teotihuacán	When the city flourished: _____ When the Aztecs first came: _____ Number of inhabitants when the city was at its height: _____ When the ruins became a World Heritage Site: _____ Why the site is important: _____ What started the current controversy: _____
Protester's main points	
Employee's main points	
Shopper's main points	

Responding to the Listening

Discuss the questions in small groups.

1. Is some kind of compromise possible between those who are for the Wal-Mart and those who are against it? If so, what would that compromise be? If not, why isn't a compromise possible?

2. Would you be willing to put up with certain inconveniences in order to preserve a cultural, natural, or historical site? Why?

3. Suppose you were living near Teotihuacán. Would you shop at the new Wal-Mart? Why?

4. What actions can be taken to preserve traditional ways, monuments, and artifacts that are in danger of being lost or destroyed?

5. Why might different age groups have differing views on the value of preserving cultural traditions and artifacts?

WORDS AND PHRASES ABOUT CULTURAL HERITAGE

Work with a partner. Read the row of words and phrases below each numbered word. One word or phrase does not describe the numbered word. Cross it out. When you are done, write your own definition for each word on the lines below. Use a dictionary to check your definition.

1. **archaeology**

   | study of ancient societies | examination of remains | recovering evidence | gerontology |

2. **artifacts**

   | objects | remains | locations | relics |

3. **assimilation**

   | being part of | segregation | absorption | integration |

4. **expatriate**

   | migrant | exile | native | émigré |

5. **gentrification**

   | upgrading | restoration | displacement of people | low-income housing |

   archaeology: _____

   artifacts: _____

   assimilation: _____

   expatriate: _____

   gentrification: _____

Work with a partner. Match the idioms on the left with their definitions on the right. Write the letter on the line. Use a dictionary if necessary.

1. _____ living in the past
2. _____ break with tradition
3. _____ a time-honored custom
4. _____ the spirit of a time/place/group

a. a way of doing something that has existed for a long time

b. thinking too much about the past, or having old-fashioned ideas and attitudes

c. the set of ideas, beliefs, and feelings that are typical of a particular period in history, a place, or a group of people

d. to change the way things have always been done in the past

Work with a partner. Use the words and phrases about cultural heritage to complete the conversation. Student A reads a sentence. Student B completes the sentence with a word or phrase. After completing four or five items, switch roles. When you are done, practice reading aloud the dialogue with your partner.

1. **A:** My grandparents are not at all interested in learning about modern technology. I think it would make their lives easier, but they refuse. They don't know how much they are missing!

   B: Perhaps they are happier _____.

2. **A:** Moving away from one's native country to a new one can be difficult. It can be hard to blend into and be accepted by a new group of people.

   B: _____ can take time and may not always be desirable.

3. **A:** My cousin grew up in a very traditional household. Her parents wanted her to attend a specific school, marry a certain person, and live a certain lifestyle, just as they had done, and their parents had done before them. She did not want to. She wanted to live a different way.

   B: She wants to _____.

4. **A:** I really enjoy learning about the remains of ancient cultures and past ways of life. This is a field of study that I would like to major in when I go to college.

   B: You should take courses in _____.

5. **A:** For many families, the idea of having dinner together every night is a custom that has existed for many generations. I know my parents and grandparents both spoke fondly of traditional family dinners.

   B: In some families, dining together every night is a _____.

6. **A:** When I return to my hometown, I am always amazed by the change. Much of the housing has been renovated and many of the people who used to live in town have had to move elsewhere. My hometown has become a very expensive place to live.

   B: Your hometown is undergoing _____.

7. **A:** I have always wanted to leave my home country and live permanently in another part of the world.

   B: You want to be an _____.

8. **A:** I am fascinated by the remnants of ancient cultures and civilizations. We can learn a lot about the past by studying cultural objects that were made and used long ago.

   B: You can learn a lot by studying cultural _____.

9. **A:** I like ancient Greek art. It gives me a sense of what life was like at that time and place in the past.

   B: Yes, such ancient art evokes the _____ of ancient _____.

PROBLEM SOLVING

Read and listen to each problem. Then look at the possible solutions given and add one or two of your own. Decide what you would do in each case. Write the reasons for your decision.

Problem 1

You are traveling in Greece and visiting an ancient site. You come across a tiny chip of a sculpture, which is probably thousands of years old. A sign instructs tourists not to remove *anything* from the site. You would like to take it home with you. What do you do?

1. Keep it because it's only a small chip.
2. Leave it where you found it and inform someone.
3. _____
4. _____

Reasons: _____
_____

Problem 2

City planners want to build a public school on a site where a key historical event occurred during the American Revolution. Some citizens feel that it is more important to build the school than to preserve the historic site. What course of action do you suggest?

1. Build the school and destroy the site.
2. Preserve the site, and build the school in another location.
3. _____
4. _____

Reasons: _____
_____

Problem 3

You and your spouse are planning to adopt a child from another country. The child you will adopt is obviously from a cultural background different from yours; his or her physical characteristics are noticeably different. One of you wants to raise the child according to your own cultural traditions; the other thinks you should raise the child with an understanding of the culture he or she came from. What do you do?

1. Raise the child to have an equal appreciation and knowledge of both cultures; the child would learn more than one language and observe more than one set of customs and beliefs.

2. Raise the child solely according to your own cultural traditions; the child would learn the language you speak and observe beliefs and customs similar to your own.

3. _____

4. _____

Reasons: _____

_____

Work in small groups. Talk about each of the previous problems and decide what your group would do. Try to use some of the words and phrases about cultural heritage on pages 129–130.

FROM THE NEWS

Preparing to Read

Answer the questions before you read. Discuss your answers as a class.

1. What kinds of changes have you observed in parts of your city or town, for example, in the makeup of the population or types of housing?

2. Why do some people feel resentful when their neighborhoods change?

Rome Loses Some Traditional Flavor

By Charles Hawley, Contributor to the
Christian Science Monitor

ROME—It used to be that some **residents** of Trastevere, a traditional working-class neighborhood on the west bank of the Tiber River, would **boast** that they had never crossed the river into central Rome. What for, after all? The **tightknit** community had everything it needed—a butcher, a baker, artisans, and, on the central square, a large vegetable market for fresh artichokes, Parmesan cheese, and garlic. It had been that way for centuries.

These days, however, Trastevere is changing. The area's new residents—young professionals, students, and, increasingly, American expatriates—go to the cocktail bar instead of the butcher and to fashion boutiques rather than bakeries. They not only scooter across the Tiber, but also jet across the Atlantic.

And the market in Trastevere, like many of the traditional **open-air** markets that define urban life in Rome, is threatening to disappear.

"The longer I had my vegetable stand, the worse business got," says Armanda Panichi, who recently gave up her stall and retired. "I get much more money from my pension than I was earning toward the end. You just can't survive on the couple of apples the tourists buy."

The changes Ms. Panichi **succumbed** to are affecting many neighborhoods in Rome, and larger cities across both Italy and Europe. Call it a collision of lifestyles or expectations: Young professionals, who are moving into the area, enjoy the **quaintness** of the outdoor markets, but don't **patronize** them. They want a modern lifestyle, which includes large supermarkets.

As a result, centrally located neighborhoods are becoming more and more trendy and—in cities like London, Paris, and Berlin, as well as Rome— are getting expensive. So far, the development is one that many European cities are encouraging, says Rowland Atkinson, a gentrification expert from the University of Glasgow.

"In North America," he says, "the word *gentrification* has very much a negative **connotation**—people immediately think of the social dislocation that often goes along with the process. In Europe, that negative connotation isn't really there yet. In England, at least, it is seen as a very positive development, as a way to combat inner city blight."

The trick, of course, is to improve the city center without sacrificing those elements that make life there unique.

Rome is becoming a city of immigrants. More than 17 percent of the 80,000 city-center residents are foreigners, and the area around the main train station is quickly developing into a Chinatown.

The percentage of foreigners in sought-after neighborhoods like Trastevere is even higher— and they tend to be richer. Two private universities in Trastevere, John Cabot University and the American University, have brought a number of American students and professors into the area. The neighborhood has also proven popular among the increasing numbers of young European professionals moving to Rome. With them have come cocktail bars, pizzerias, cafes, and stylish shops. On weekend evenings, the narrow, cobblestone streets of Trastevere are jammed with young partiers enjoying the old-city atmosphere.

Yet what they are looking for is quickly disappearing, says Bjorn Thomassen, a professor of anthropology at the American University who is planning to teach a course next term on Rome's gentrification.

"It is a bit **ironic**," he says, "that Trastevere is sort of the heart of Rome, and many people, Romans included, talk about it being the real Rome. But there aren't too many Romans there anymore. They are all moving out."

And they are taking their traditions with them.

For centuries, Romans have made daily market visits to pick over the colorful bounty of fruits, vegetables, and cheeses piled up on the wooden tables under broad sun umbrellas. But today, those who have moved into central Rome are more likely to shop after working hours at the growing number of supermarkets that dot central Rome than at the open-air markets.

Help may be on the way, according to Giovanni Pineschi, an urban planner working on an independent evaluation of Rome's transportation network. After decades of allowing more or less uncontrolled growth with no effort to retain traditional shops and lifestyles, the Roman government is now pursuing a "master plan" aimed at preserving the character of central neighborhoods. But, he says, there probably won't be assistance available to older residents of neighborhoods like Trastevere.

For the Trastevere market vendors, about all they can hope for is that their new neighbors get used to shopping out of doors. Bruno Valentini, a fruit-stall operator who lives on the outskirts of Rome, is hoping that the city pays for **refurbishing** the market's run-down sales booths, or replaces them entirely.

"We definitely need help to compete," says Mr. Valentini. "We could really attract more customers if our stalls looked nice and were more traditional. But the city doesn't seem to care."

Checking Your Comprehension

Write your responses to the following items according to the information and opinions in the news article.

1. What kind of neighborhood was Trastevere before it began to change?

   _____

2. What kinds of changes are taking place in Trastevere today? Describe the changes to the local population, the open-air markets, and the cost of living in the neighborhood.

   _____

3. Why does the word *gentrification* sometimes have a negative connotation?

   _____

4. How is the arrival of young professionals affecting neighborhoods in Rome?

   _____

5. How has the population of Rome itself changed?

   _____

6. How are the new residents of Rome different from the older residents when it comes to shopping?

   _____

7. What is the Roman government doing to help preserve Trastevere?

   _____

8. What can the vendors of Trastevere hope for?

   _____

Thinking Critically About the Reading

Discuss in small groups. Then share your responses with the class.

1. Are changes like the ones that are occurring in Trastevere inevitable and unavoidable? Why?

2. Do you agree with Rowland Atkinson that gentrification has a negative connotation in North America? Explain your reasoning.

3. If you moved to a place like Trastevere with a strong tradition, would you want to maintain it or modernize it? Why?

4. What is negative about the changes occurring in Trastevere? What is positive about them?

WORDS AND PHRASES FROM THE READING

Look at the words in the box. Find them in boldface print in the news article on page 133. Look at the context of each word. Can you figure out the meaning?

boast	connotation	ironic	open-air	patronize
quaintness	refurbishing	residents	succumbed	tightknit

Fill in the crossword puzzle using the words in the box. Use a dictionary if necessary.

Down

1. thoroughly repairing and improving a building
2. people who live or stay in a place such as a house, town, or country
4. happening or existing outdoors, not in a building
5. to use or visit a store or restaurant
6. closely connected with each other
7. amusing or unusual because something strange happens or the opposite of what was expected happens or is true
9. stopped opposing someone or something stronger and allowed it to take control

Across

3. to talk too proudly about your possessions, abilities, or achievements; brag
8. the quality of being unusual and attractive in an old-fashioned way
10. a feeling or an idea that a word makes you think of

Read the sentences. Circle the best definition for each underlined phrase.

1. Even though the new residents of Trastevere like the charm of the traditional open-air markets, they prefer to shop at modern establishments, such as large supermarkets. Some people view this as a <u>collision of lifestyles</u>.
   a. a clash between two ways of life
   b. the integration of two ways of life

2. Sometimes when a traditional town or village undergoes modernization, long-time residents are forced out, have to move elsewhere, and lose touch with one another. This type of <u>social dislocation</u> is a negative aspect of gentrification.
   a. the act, process, or state of being put out of your usual social place or position
   b. the act, process, or state of being indifferent or hostile

3. In many city centers, which are often the older areas of a town, buildings are sometimes in disrepair. The residents often welcome changes such as new stores opening and new neighbors moving in. They feel it will help improve the <u>inner city blight</u> that often exists.
   a. the part of a city, near the middle, where the buildings have been renovated and the people are often rich
   b. the part of a city, near the middle, where the buildings are in a bad condition and the people are often poor

4. Many wealthy foreigners want to live in Trastevere. It has become a popular and <u>sought-after</u> place to live.
   a. hard to locate because the streets are narrow and intricate
   b. wanted by a lot of people, but rare or difficult to get

Idioms with *Run*

In English, there are many idioms and phrases that contain the word run, each with its own meaning. For example, in the news article, the adjective run-down means "in a very bad condition." Below are other common phrases and idioms with run. Look at the list and think about the meaning of each expression.

run across	run out of
run after	run through
run errands	run up
run in the family	run up against

Work with a partner to complete the statements using the expressions above. Use a dictionary if necessary.

1. Many people in my family enjoy studying languages. An ability to learn languages easily is something that seems to _____.

2. When I visit another country, I am more than happy to go to the store, the post office, and the bank; I enjoy just being out and about in a new and different place. I am always happy to _____.

3. In Rome, I found an interesting shop that sells copies of unusual artwork. I was not even looking for the store but just happened to find it. I was happy to _____ it.

4. I always want to learn something new; I am very curious about other cultures. I never seem to _____ curiosity!

5. Traveling, while fun, can be very expensive. Last time I traveled, I spent a lot more money than I had planned. I didn't plan to _____ my credit card bill, but I did.

6. The removal of artifacts from a country is a serious crime. People who try to remove art and other artifacts will _____ public resistance and legal challenges.

7. I studied traditional dance last year. At the end of the class, we performed. We rehearsed a lot before the show. We had to _____ the dances many times until we had them right.

8. I was videotaping a procession in a small town when I had to stop and reload my camera. The procession moved so fast I had to _____ them to catch up. I didn't want to miss anything!

CONVERSATION TIP

Certain words and phrases can help you describe a process to someone else. They help the listener follow each step in the process as you talk. Here are some examples of words and phrases you can use to describe the beginning, middle, and end of a process.

Describing a Process

Beginning	During	End
You begin by . . .	An important step is . . .	Once everything else has been done, then you . . .
To start off . . .	Once you have done that, then you . . .	Finally, you . . .
First you . . .	After that you . . .	To top it all off . . .
The initial step is . . .	Next you . . .	The final step is . . .
Before you can do anything, you have to . . .	Following that . . .	Last but not least . . .
The first thing is to . . .	The next thing is to . . .	At the very end . . .

ACT IT OUT

Describe the preparation of a traditional food in your culture, including the ingredients you need to buy and the steps involved in making the dish itself.

Write down each step and present them in a logical, step-by-step order. Use phrases that will make the order of the steps clear to someone else. Also, try to include vivid adjectives in your description so that your audience will be able to imagine the colors, smells, tastes, and sounds involved in the preparation of the food.

When you are ready, describe the preparation of the food or meal to a group of four other students. Take turns describing your dishes until everyone has had a turn.

> *Sushi is one of my favorite traditional foods. Before you can do anything, you'll need to have the right tools—a bamboo rolling mat called a makisu, a cutting board, and a sharp knife. Next, you will need to buy the ingredients: medium grain rice, rice vinegar, sugar, nori seaweed, wasabi (a green, spicy Japanese horseradish mustard), gari (pickled, thinly sliced ginger), extremely fresh fish and other seafood, cucumber, avocado, and other vegetables, depending upon what type of sushi you plan to make, and soy sauce.*

SAYINGS ABOUT CULTURE

Read and discuss the meaning of each quotation in small groups and compare the sayings to your own ideas about "culture."

◆ *No culture can live, if it attempts to be exclusive.*

—Mahatma Gandhi
(Indian spiritual/political leader and humanitarian, 1869–1948)

◆ *Tolerance, inter-cultural dialogue and respect for diversity are more essential than ever in a world where peoples are becoming more and more closely interconnected.*

—Kofi Annan
(Ghanian-born Secretary-General of the United Nations, b. 1938)

◆ *I do not want my house to be walled in on all sides and my windows to be stuffed. I want the cultures of all the lands to be blown about my house as freely as possible. But I refuse to be blown off my feet by any.*

—Mahatma Gandhi

◆ *Culture [is] the acquainting ourselves with the best that has been known and said in the world, and thus with the history of the human spirit.*

—Matthew Arnold
(English poet and critic, 1822–1888)

◆ *That is true culture which helps us to work for the social betterment of all.*

—Henry Ward Beecher
(American abolitionist and clergyman, 1813–1887)

Discuss with group members your reaction to each quotation. Then discuss what "culture" means to you. According to one dictionary definition, culture means "the ideas, beliefs, and customs that are shared by people in a society." Do you agree with this definition? Work with your group to come up with your own definition or saying about "culture." When you are done, share your group's definition or saying with the rest of the class.

BEYOND THE CLASSROOM

Continue to explore the unit theme by completing the following activities.

1. Many countries such as Greece, Turkey, Italy, and China are rich in artifacts. Unfortunately, some of the artifacts from these countries have been removed and are displayed in museums in other countries. Use the Internet to research a country that has a high incidence of artifact removal. Find out who is removing the artifacts and where they are being taken and why. Investigate what different groups are saying and doing about the situation. What are the arguments in favor of bringing the artifacts back to the original country? What are the arguments for allowing the artifacts to remain elsewhere? Write a short essay that answers some or all of these questions, and express your own feelings about the situation.

2. Do some online research about places throughout the world that have been designated as World Heritage sites by the United Nations. Pick one place that interests you. Write a short descriptive essay about the site. Describe what the site is like, why it is in danger, and what is being done to preserve it. Give a short oral report to the class based on your essay. If possible, include some photographs of the site in your essay and oral report.

APPENDIX: WORDS AND PHRASES

a dime a dozen (7)
a good sport (2)
a steal (3)
a time-honored custom (12)
a touch of (11)
abuse (2)
adopted (6)
alleviate (9)
amoral (2)
ancestor (8)
anonymous (4)
appeal (5)
archaeology (12)
aristocracy (7)
artifacts (12)
assimilation (12)
astute (7)
at your fingertips (1)
atmosphere (2)
attire (6)
authorities (4)
automatically (1)
be hard pressed (9)
be on a shoestring (7)
behind closed doors (1)
big draw (9)
blog (9)
blood relation (8)
boast (12)
break with tradition (12)
can't take their eyes off (5)
catch a glimpse of (5)
categories (1)
caught by surprise (11)
championship (2)
charitable foundation (10)
chat room (9)
chic (6)
Chief Executive Officer (10)

claims (5)
clamor (2)
classified (1)
cloud sound judgment (2)
codes of professional ethics (4)
coercion (11)
collegiality (10)
collision of lifestyles (12)
computer crash (9)
condition (11)
conducted (3)
confidential (1)
conjures up (6)
connotation (12)
conscientious (4)
consequences (4)
constructive (2)
consumer (1)
cooperative (10)
cosmetics (6)
counteract (3)
cyberspace (9)
deals (3)
dedication (2)
deficiencies (11)
demeanor (6)
descendants(8)
deterioration (4)
detriment (8)
diagnosed (11)
dilemma (11)
diminish (11)
distorts (11)
domestic (8)
downside (6)
dress down (6)
dress up (6)
eavesdrop (1)
economize (3)

edition (1)
effect (3)
elective (11)
emigrants (7)
endemic (5)
enlisted (9)
enterprise (5)
enthusiasts (9)
entrepreneurial (7)
Equal Employment
    Opportunity (10)
ethical conduct (10)
evening wear (6)
executive (10)
expatriate (12)
exposing (4)
extended family (8)
extravagant (3)
fall back into (8)
fall guy (4)
fashion plate (6)
fashion statement (6)
forged alliances (10)
free expression (6)
free markets (2)
frugal (3)
fuel the success of (5)
gawk (5)
genealogy (9)
gentrification (12)
get rid of (4)
getting a kick out of (5)
gifted (2)
glance (5)
go for it (6)
graphics (9)
gratification (2)
gross (10)
ground rules (8)

guarantee (10)

hardware (9)

heads up (1)

Health Maintenance
Organization (10)

help lines (9)

hit it off (9)

hoard (7)

Human Resources (10)

hush-hush (1)

identified (1)

increase (3)

indicates (3)

indisputably (7)

inevitable (11)

infamy (2)

informer (4)

infringe on (1)

in-laws (8)

inner city blight (12)

innovation (7)

inserting (1)

inspiring (5)

instantly (1)

instigator (10)

instituted (6)

integrity (2)

interest groups (10)

intimacy (1)

invasion of privacy (1)

ironic (12)

isolation (9)

justified (4)

keep it to yourself (1)

know-how (3)

launched (5)

let the cat out of the bag (4)

living in the past (12)

living the high life (7)

lose sight of (8)

mandatory (6)

marked down (3)

matriarchal (8)

means (7)

medical emergencies (5)

medication (1)

merchandise (3)

misconduct (4)

mishaps (5)

mom-and-pop (10)

momentum (11)

moral compass (4)

morbid curiosity (5)

motives (10)

multinational corporation (10)

multitasking (9)

natural disasters (5)

nest egg (7)

next frontier (11)

none of your business (1)

normally (3)

notion (9)

nuclear family (8)

nurtured (8)

open-air (12)

open ended (8)

operations (10)

originate (10)

patriarchal (8)

patronize (12)

peer (5)

perpetrated (6)

physical (6)

pioneered (7)

potential (8)

Preferred Provider
Organization (10)

prescription (11)

procedure (11)

promotions (3)

prone to (11)

proportion (7)

public company (10)

published (3)

pull together (8)

pursuit (9)

quaintness (12)

raising the issue (11)

ranges (9)

reference point (3)

reflexes (11)

refurbishing (12)

reluctant (1)

remnant (7)

reprisals (4)

resentful (6)

residents (12)

resilient (8)

restrictive (6)

retaliation (4)

rip-off (3)

risk takers (7)

rough and ready (7)

rubbernecking (5)

run across (12)

run after (12)

run errands (12)

run in the family (12)

run out of (12)

run the gamut (8)

run through (12)

run up (12)

run up against (12)

sacrifice (2)

scandal (4)

scanner (1)

scrutinized (2)

search engine (9)

sectors (7)

self-imposed (2)

self-made (7)

sell like hotcakes (3)

set aside (7)

shape the future (11)

shareholder (10)

shortcuts (2)

shortsighted (2)

side effects (11)

single-parent family (8)

skepticism (6)

snail mail (9)

social dislocation (12)

software (9)

sought after (12)

spam (9)

spanned (3)

spare no expense (7)

spared (11)

specialist (11)

spectator (5)

spendthrift (7)

squander (3)

stamina (2)

standards (5)

status (8)

stick to them (3)

stingy (7)

strict guidelines (11)

subscribers (5)

succumbed (12)

suppress (4)

surfing the Net/Web (9)

symptoms (11)

take to (9)

tentative (8)

the playing field is level (2)

the spirit of a time/
   place/group (12)

the trenches (6)

theoretical musings (11)

thrive on (6)

tightknit (12)

to get the ax (4)

to name names (4)

to rat on (4)

to take the rap (4)

tolerate (4)

track (1)

traits (8)

trend (8)

trendy (6)

triumph (2)

turmoil (8)

under the weather (11)

unethical (4)

upward mobility (7)

virtual (9)

virus (9)

vision (10)

voyeuristic (5)

weigh in on (2)

win by a narrow margin (2)

window shopping (3)

won hands down (2)

words of caution (11)

words of wisdom (3)

wring their hands (2)

zip on through (1)

CONVERSATION TIPS

UNIT 1 page 11

Using Enthusiasm to Persuade

I've got a fantastic idea . . .
I think it'd be a great idea to . . .
Doesn't this sound good?
What do you think about . . .
Why don't we . . .
I'm almost certain you'll go along with me on this . . .

Responding to Someone Else's Idea

Declining

That sounds good, but I don't think so.
I really don't think so because . . .
No thanks, I'd rather not.
I don't know . . .

Accepting

Sure, that sounds great.
I'd love to.
Count me in!
Why not!

UNIT 2 page 24

Leading and Taking Part in Discussions

Leading/Facilitating

Who would like to begin?
What do you think about . . . ?
Would someone else like to comment on that?
What is your response?
Is there another side to the issue?
Does someone have another point to make?

Entering/Participating

First of all, I'd like to say that . . .
I'd like to begin by saying that . . .
I agree/disagree with that position because . . .
We should also consider the opposing view . . .
I'd like to add to what was said so far.
I want to take another perspective on . . .

UNIT 3 page 35

Saying "No" to a Salesperson

Formal

Excuse me, but no thank you.
I beg your pardon, but I am not looking for . . .
I appreciate your help, but no.
No, thank you. I'm just looking/ browsing/window shopping.

Informal

Thanks, but I'm really not interested.
Not today, but thanks anyway.

UNIT 4 page 45

Confronting a Difficult Situation

We need to talk.
I've got something I need to say.
I am not sure how to say this but . . .
This is really difficult to say.
You may not want to hear this but . . .
I'm sorry but I really need to say this.

UNIT 5 page 56

Expressing Disapproval

Formal/Polite

I find this . . .
   objectionable
   distasteful
   offensive
   too graphic
   off-putting
   disgraceful

Informal/Slang

This is really . . .
   gross
   revolting
   foul
This turns my stomach
   sickens me
   disgusts me

UNIT 6 page 66

Speaking About Disappointment

Expressing Disappointment

I was really looking forward to . . .
I really had my mind set on . . .
It's too bad that . . .
I'm disappointed that . . .
I'm troubled because . . .
I feel crushed.

Reacting to Disappointment

Sorry to hear that.
That's too bad/a shame.
Sometimes these things happen.
It's out of your control.
Try not to take it personally.
Things have a way of working out.

Offering Another View

You could always . . .
Look at it this way . . .
It could be worse. What if you had to . . .
In the overall scheme of things, it's not as bad as you think.

UNIT 7 page 77

Showing Surprise and Disbelief

You're kidding!/You've got to be kidding!
Why would you . . . ?
That's staggering news.
That's beyond belief.
I'm astounded/amazed/taken aback.

Responding to Surprise and Disbelief

I know it is difficult to believe, but it's true.
I'm not making this up.
I've thought it through and this is my decision.
The reality is . . .
It's a fact.
Take my word for it.

UNIT 8   page 89

Expressing Determination

This is what I have decided to do
I've made up my mind.
There's no talking me out of this.
I am determined to . . .
I've thought long and hard
about this.
There is nothing you can say to
change my mind.
It's a done deal.
I'm sticking to my guns about this.

UNIT 9   page 99

Giving Your Perspective

Formal

From my perspective . . .
One way to look at it is . . .
On the other hand

Informal

The way I see it is . . .
Look at it this way
If you ask me . . .

UNIT 10   page 110

Interviewing Dos and Dont's

Do

Be brief and to the point
Describe experiences positively
Turn weaknesses into strengths
Ask for clarification of vague
questions
Be courteous
Mention specific skills and
experiences
Support statements with examples
Remember the question while
answering
Be active, involved, and enthuastic, and
ask questions
Find out when the company will make
the decision and notify candidates, and
follow up accordingly

Don't

Ramble or talk too much
Blame past employers or criticize
others
Dwell on weaknesses, saying too
much
Guess at a meaning, or fake a
response
Interrupt
Expect the résumé to speak for you
Answer just "yes" or "no"
Ramble, then ask, "What was the
question?"
Be passive or boring
Sit around waiting for a call

Typical Interview Questions

Tell us a little about yourself.
Why are you interested in working for
this company?
What has been your greatest
accomplishment?
Describe your greatest strengths and
weaknesses.
What did you like best and least about
your previous job?
Give an example of a problem you
faced on the job, and how you solved it.
Describe a time when you were faced
with problems or stressful situations at
work. What did you do to improve the
situation?
What would you like to be doing five
years from now?
Would you rather be in charge of a
project or work as part of a team?
What have you learned from the jobs
you have held?

UNIT 11   page 124

Questions to Ask Your Doctor Before You Have Surgery

1. What operation are you
   recommending?
2. Why do I need the surgery?
3. Can you explain the surgery to me?
   Will something be removed or
   repaired? If so, what?
4. Why is the surgery necessary?

5. Are there alternative ways to
   perform the surgery? If so, what are
   they and what are their benefits and
   risks?
6. What are the benefits of surgery?
   How long will the benefits last?
7. What are the risks of surgery?
8. What happens if I choose to not
   have the surgery?
9. Are you experienced in performing
   this surgery? Please explain.
10. How long will I stay in the
    hospital?
11. What kind of anesthesia will
    I need?
12. How long will it take me to
    recover?
13. How much will the surgery cost?
    Will my insurance company pay
    part or all of the expense?
14. Where can I get a second opinion?

UNIT 12   page 137

Describing a Process

Beginning

You begin by . . .
To start off . . .
First you . . .
The initial step is . . .
Before you can do anything, you
have to . . .
The first thing is to . . .

During

An important step is . . .
Once you have done that, then you . . .
After that you
Next you . . .
Following that . . .
The next thing is to . . .

End

Once everything else has been done,
then you . . .
Finally, you . . .
To top it all off . . .
The final step is . . .
Last but not least . . .
At the very end . . .